DATE DUE

AP 9 '97			
OC 9 '97			
OC 19 '98			
OC 05 '04			

DEMCO 38-297

THE
SANTEE SIOUX

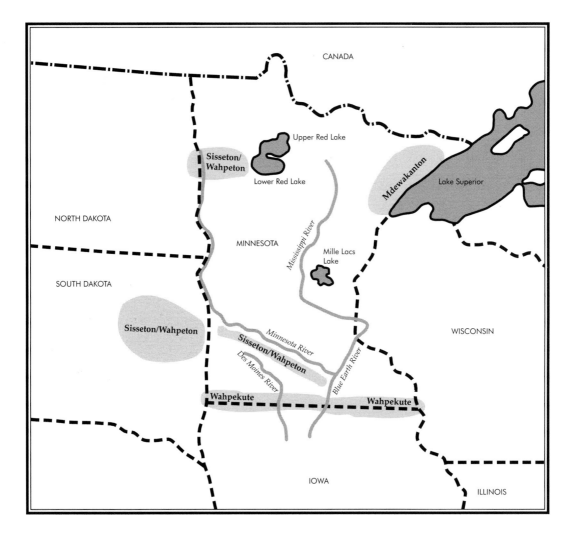

INDIANS OF NORTH AMERICA

THE
SANTEE SIOUX

Nancy Bonvillain

Frank W. Porter III
General Editor

CHELSEA HOUSE PUBLISHERS
Philadelphia

On the Cover Front view of a fringed deerskin jacket probably made by Nebraska Santee women, circa 1890.

Frontis: This map shows where different bands of the Santee Sioux tribe lived in what would later become the Minnesota Territory. After the failed Sioux uprising of 1862, the Santees were driven from their beloved "Big Woods" almost entirely.

Chelsea House Publishers
Editorial Director Richard Rennert
Picture Editor Judy Hasday
Art Director Sara Davis
Production Manager Pamela Loos

Indians of North America
Senior Editor John Ziff

Staff for **THE SANTEE SIOUX**
Associate Editor Therese DeAngelis
Editorial Assistant Kristine Brennan
Designer Cambraia Magalhaes
Picture Research Alan Gotlieb

First Printing

1 3 5 7 9 8 6 4 2

Libraray of Congress Cataloging-in-Publication Data

Bonvillain, Nancy.
      The Santee Sioux / Nancy Bonvillain.
             p. cm.—(Indians of North America)
      Includes bibliographical references and index.
      Summary: Presents a history of one division of Dakota Indians of the northern plains and prairies including their traditions, the impact of reservations, and current way of life.
      ISBN 0-7910-1685-4
        0-7910-3482-8 (pbk.)
      1. Santee Indians—Juvenile literature. [1. Santee Indians. 2. Indians of North America.] I. Title. II. Series: Indians of North America (Chelsea House Publishers)
E99. S22B66 1996
973'.04975—dc20   95-31524
                                     CIP
                                     AC

CONTENTS

INDIANS OF NORTH AMERICA

CHELSEA HOUSE PUBLISHERS

INDIANS OF NORTH AMERICA: CONFLICT AND SURVIVAL

Frank W. Porter III

The Indians survived our open intention of wiping them out, and since the tide turned they have even weathered our good intentions toward them, which can be much more deadly.

John Steinbeck
America and Americans

When Europeans first reached the North American continent, they found hundreds of tribes occupying a vast and rich country. The newcomers quickly recognized the wealth of natural resources. They were not, however, so quick or willing to recognize the spiritual, cultural, and intellectual riches of the people they called Indians.

The Indians of North America examines the problems that develop when people with different cultures come together. For American Indians, the consequences of their interaction with non-Indian people have been both productive and tragic. The Europeans believed they had "discovered" a "New World," but their religious bigotry, cultural bias, and materialistic world view kept them from appreciating and understanding the people who lived in it. All too often they attempted to change the way of life of the indigenous people. The Spanish conquistadores wanted the Indians as a source of labor. The Christian missionaries, many of whom were English, viewed them as potential converts. French traders and trappers used the Indians as a means to obtain pelts. As Francis Parkman, the 19th-century historian, stated, "Spanish civilization crushed the Indian; English civilization scorned and neglected him; French civilization embraced and cherished him."

Nearly 500 years later, many people think of American Indians as curious vestiges of a distant past, waging a futile war to survive in a Space Age society. Even today, our understanding of the history and culture of American Indians is too often derived from unsympathetic, culturally biased, and inaccurate reports. The American Indian, described and portrayed in thousands of movies, television programs, books, articles, and government studies, has either been raised to the status of the "noble savage" or disparaged as the "wild Indian" who resisted the westward expansion of the American frontier.

Where in this popular view are the real Indians, the human beings and communities whose ancestors can be traced back to ice-age hunters? Where are the creative and indomitable people whose sophisticated technologies used the natural resources to ensure their survival, whose military skill might even have prevented European settlement of North America if not for devastating epidemics and the disruption of the ecology? Where are the men and women who are today diligently struggling to assert their legal rights and express once again the value of their heritage?

The various Indian tribes of North America, like people everywhere, have a history that includes population expansion, adaptation to a range of regional environments, trade across wide networks, internal strife, and warfare. This was the reality. Europeans justified their conquests, however, by creating a mythical image of the New World and its native people. In this myth, the New World was a virgin land, waiting for the Europeans. The arrival of Christopher Columbus ended a timeless primitiveness for the original inhabitants.

Also part of this myth was the debate over the origins of the American Indians. Fantastic and diverse answers were proposed by the early explorers, missionaries, and settlers. Some thought that the Indians were descended from the Ten Lost Tribes of Israel, others that they were descended from inhabitants of the lost continent of Atlantis. One writer suggested that the Indians had reached North America in another Noah's ark.

A later myth, perpetrated by many historians, focused on the relentless persecution during the past five centuries until only a scattering of these "primitive" people remained to be herded onto reservations. This view fails to chronicle the overt and covert ways in which the Indians successfully coped with the intruders.

All of these myths presented one-sided interpretations that ignored the complexity of European and American events and policies. All left serious questions unanswered. What were the origins of the American Indians? Where did they come from? How and when did they get to the New World? What was their life—their culture—really like?

In the late 1800s, anthropologists and archaeologists in the Smithsonian Institution's newly created Bureau of American Ethnology in Washington, D. C., began to study scientifically the history and culture of the Indians of North America. They were motivated by an honest belief that the Indians were on the verge of extinction and that along with them would vanish their languages, religious beliefs, technology, myths, and legends. These men and women went out to visit, study, and record data from as many Indian communities as possible before this information was forever lost.

By this time there was a new myth in the national consciousness. American Indians existed as figures in the American past. They had performed a historical mission. They had challenged white settlers who trekked across the continent. Once conquered, however, they were supposed to accept graciously the way of life of their conquerors.

The reality again was different. American Indians resisted both actively and passively. They refused to lose their unique identity, to be assimilated into white society. Many whites viewed the Indians not only as members of a conquered nation but also as "inferior" and "unequal." The rights of the Indians could be expanded, contracted, or modified as the conquerors saw fit. In every generation, white society asked itself what to do with the American Indians. Their answers have resulted in the twists and turns of federal Indian policy.

There were two general approaches. One way was to raise the Indians to a "higher level" by "civilizing" them. Zealous missionaries considered it their Christian duty to elevate the Indian through conversion and scanty education. The other approach was to ignore the Indians until they disappeared under pressure from the ever-expanding white society. The myth of the "vanishing Indian" gave stronger support to the latter option, helping to justify the taking of the Indians' land.

Prior to the end of the 18th century, there was no national policy on Indians simply because the American nation had not yet come into existence. American Indians similarly did not possess a political or social unity with which to confront the various Europeans. They were not homogeneous. Rather, they were loosely formed bands and tribes, speaking nearly 300 languages and thousands of dialects. The collective identity felt by Indians today is a result of their common experiences of defeat and/or mistreatment at the hands of whites.

During the colonial period, the British crown did not have a coordinated policy toward the Indians of North America. Specific tribes (most notably the Iroquois and the Cherokee) became military and political pawns used by both the crown and the individual colonies. The success of the American Revolution brought no immediate change. When the United States acquired new territory from France and Mexico in the early 19th century, the federal government wanted to open this land to settlement by homesteaders. But the Indian tribes that lived on this land had signed treaties with European governments assuring their title to the land. Now the United States assumed legal responsibility for honoring these treaties.

At first, President Thomas Jefferson believed that the Louisiana Purchase contained sufficient land for both the Indians and the white population.

Within a generation, though, it became clear that the Indians would not be allowed to remain. In the 1830s the federal government began to coerce the eastern tribes to sign treaties agreeing to relinquish their ancestral land and move west of the Mississippi River. Whenever these negotiations failed, President Andrew Jackson used the military to remove the Indians. The southeastern tribes, promised food and transportation during their removal to the West, were instead forced to walk the "Trail of Tears." More than 4,000 men, women, and children died during this forced march. The "removal policy" was successful in opening the land to homesteaders, but it created enormous hardships for the Indians.

By 1871 most of the tribes in the United States had signed treaties ceding most or all of their ancestral land in exchange for reservations and welfare. The treaty terms were intended to bind both parties for all time. But in the General Allotment Act of 1887, the federal government changed its policy again. Now the goal was to make tribal members into individual landowners and farmers, encouraging their absorption into white society. This policy was advantageous to whites who were eager to acquire Indian land, but it proved disastrous for the Indians. One hundred thirty-eight million acres of reservation land were subdivided into tracts of 160, 80, or as little as 40 acres, and allotted to tribe members on an individual basis. Land owned in this way was said to have "trust status" and could not be sold. But the surplus land—all Indian land not allotted to individuals— was opened (for sale) to white settlers. Ultimately, more than 90 million acres of land were taken from the Indians by legal and illegal means.

The resulting loss of land was a catastrophe for the Indians. It was necessary to make it illegal for Indians to sell their land to non-Indians. The Indian Reorganization Act of 1934 officially ended the allotment period. Tribes that voted to accept the provisions of this act were reorganized, and an effort was made to purchase land within preexisting reservations to restore an adequate land base.

Ten years later, in 1944, federal Indian policy again shifted. Now the federal government wanted to get out of the "Indian business." In 1953 an act of Congress named specific tribes whose trust status was to be ended "at the earliest possible time." This new law enabled the United States to end unilaterally, whether the Indians wished it or not, the special status that protected the land in Indian tribal reservations. In the 1950s federal Indian policy was to transfer federal responsibility and jurisdiction to state governments, encourage the physical relocation of Indian peoples from reservations to urban areas, and hasten the termination, or extinction, of tribes.

Between 1954 and 1962 Congress passed specific laws authorizing the termination of more than 100 tribal groups. The stated purpose of the termination policy was to ensure the full and complete integration of Indians into American society. However, there is a less benign way to interpret this legislation. Even as termination was being discussed in Congress, 133 separate bills were introduced to permit the transfer of trust land ownership from Indians to non-Indians.

With the Johnson administration in the 1960s the federal government began to reject termination. In the 1970s yet another Indian policy emerged. Known as "self-determination," it favored keeping the protective role of the federal government while increasing tribal participation in, and control of, important areas of local government. In 1983 President Reagan, in a policy statement on Indian affairs, restated the unique "government to government" relationship of the United States with the Indians. However, federal programs since then have moved toward transferring Indian affairs to individual states, which have long desired to gain control of Indian land and resources.

As long as American Indians retain power, land, and resources that are coveted by the states and the federal government, there will continue to be a "clash of cultures," and the issues will be contested in the courts, Congress, the White House, and even in the international human rights community. To give all Americans a greater comprehension of the issues and conflicts involving American Indians today is a major goal of this series. These issues are not easily understood, nor can these conflicts be readily resolved. The study of North American Indian history and culture is a necessary and important step toward that comprehension. All Americans must learn the history of the relations between the Indians and the federal government, recognize the unique legal status of the Indians, and understand the heritage and cultures of the Indians of North America.

Dr. Charles Eastman poses in his beloved Minnesota woods in 1927. A Santee by birth, Eastman was trained as a physician.

HOME
OF
THE
SANTEE
DAKOTA

Charles Eastman, a Santee physician and writer born in 1858, described the beauty and richness of his native environment in the woods of present-day Minnesota with the following words:

> Our teepees rose in clusters along the outskirts of the heavy forest that clothes the sloping side of the mountain. The rolling yellow plains were checkered with herds of buffaloes. Along the banks of the streams that ran down from the mountains were also many elk. Deer, too, were plenty, and the brooks were alive with trout. Here and there the streams were dammed by the industrious beaver.
>
> In the interior of the forest there were lakes with many islands, where moose, elk, deer, and bears were abundant. The water-fowl were wont to gather here in great numbers, among them the crane, swan, loon, and many smaller birds. Here the partridge drummed the loudest, while the whippoorwill sang with spirit, and the hooting owl reigned in the night.

The Santee lived amid the forests, mountains, lakes, and streams of Minnesota for hundreds of years. They developed their economy to make best use of their bountiful homeland and enjoyed considerable prosperity. But by the time of Eastman's birth in the middle of the 19th century, the presence of whites in Santee territory was seriously disrupting the native people's lifestyle. As a result of foreign intruders and pressures from the American government, the Santee lost nearly all of their original territory in a few short years. Today, about 7,000 Santees reside on several reservations and native communities in Minnesota, Nebraska, and the Dakotas. Some 3,000 Santees live on reserves in the Canadian provinces of Manitoba and Saskatchewan. And approximately 10,000 more Santees live away from their reservations in the United States and Canada.

The Santee are the easternmost of three divisions of Native Americans known collectively as the Sioux or Dakota. West of the Santee lived the Yankton, a central Dakota people. Still farther west were the Teton. The name of these peoples is sometimes given as *Sioux* and sometimes as *Dakota*. The word *Sioux* comes from the language of the nearby Ojibwa, who used their word *Nadoweisiweg*, or "Lesser Snakes," to label their neighbors. When French traders heard the Ojibwa word, they shortened it to *Sioux*. In the Santee's own language, the people call themselves *Dakota*, meaning "allies" or "friends." In dialects of the Teton, the word is pronounced with an *l* as Lakota. In central Yankton dialects, it is pronounced with an *n* as Nakota.

The Dakota divisions of the Santee, Teton, and Yankton refer to themselves collectively as members of the Seven Council Fires. They are distinct social and political entities, but they recognize their common culture and heritage. They speak separate dialects of the Dakota language, a member of a large family of related languages called the Siouan family. Siouan languages share many characteristics of sounds, grammar, and vocabulary. The Dakota people also share most cultural characteristics of economy, social systems, and religious beliefs. Members of the Seven Council Fires were never integrated into a stable political system or confederacy,

but they all agreed never to fight one another. They had close bonds of friendship, traded with each other, and often intermarried.

Each of the three Dakota divisions is subdivided into a number of separate groups or bands. The divisions and bands all have their own names. The name of the Santee comes from the native word *isanti*, or "knife." It refers to one of their traditional locations near Knife Lake in present-day Minnesota. The Santee's four bands are called the Wahpeton (WA-pe-ton; "dwellers among the leaves"), the Mdewakanton (mi-de-WA-kan-ton; "people of Spirit Lake"), the Wahpekute (WA-pe-koot; "shooters among the leaves"), and the Sisseton (SI-se-ton; "camping among the swamps").

The Yankton's name comes from the native word *ihanktunwan*, meaning "dwellers of the end." They have two bands, the Yankton and Yanktonai, or "little Yankton." The Teton's name is derived from *tetonwan*, meaning "dwellers of the prairie." The Teton are subdivided into several groups, including the Oglala ("they scatter their own"); the Sicangu ("burnt thighs"), sometimes referred to today as the Brulé, from the French word meaning "burnt"; the Hunkpapa ("those who camp at the entrance"); the Sihasapa ("blackfeet"); the Itazipco ("without bows"); the Oohenonpa ("two kettles"); and the Miniconjou ("those who plant by the stream").

By the middle of the 18th century, the three Dakota divisions occupied

The artist George Catlin painted this portrayal of a small Santee settlement on Lake Calhoun, near Fort Snelling, Minnesota, in 1837.

separate territories in the woodlands and prairies of what are now the states of Minnesota, North and South Dakota, and Wyoming. Each subgroup or band had its own customary lands within the division's territory. The Mdewakanton Santee lived in eastern and central Minnesota along the banks of the Mississippi River and lower portions of the Minnesota River. The Wahpekute band lived in southern Minnesota near the Blue Earth and Des Moines rivers. The Sisseton and Wahpeton Santee occupied land in western Minnesota and eastern South Dakota, on both sides of the Minnesota River and around lakes. It is likely that Santee territory extended far north and west of these locations in earlier centuries. At that

time, Santees also occupied land in the present-day Canadian provinces of Manitoba and Saskatchewan.

The central division of the Yankton Dakota lived west of the Santee from western Minnesota to the eastern banks of the Missouri River. The Teton lived still farther west along the Missouri River. Their hunting territory extended through the Dakotas and into Wyoming.

All the Dakota peoples built villages along the shores of rivers and lakes. Close to the clusters of homes, women planted gardens of corn, beans, and squash. They gathered wild rice, berries, and other plants, roots, and seeds. Men hunted animals in forests and on prairies and caught fish in numerous

Santee families in their village, as drawn by a white visitor in the early 19th century.

nearby waters. The economies of the Dakota divisions varied somewhat depending on their specific location. The Yankton and Teton relied more on farming and hunting buffalo than did the Santee, who specialized in harvesting the abundant wild rice that grew in marshy lakes throughout their territory, hunted deer and elk, and fished.

In addition to interactions among the three Dakota divisions, the Santee had frequent contact with other native peoples living nearby. The Cheyenne resided on land south and west of the Santee. And three communities of farming peoples—the Mandan, Arikara, and Hidatsa—lived along the banks of the Missouri River. The Santee had good relations with all of these peoples. They traded with the Cheyenne for buffalo hides and with the Mandan, Arikara, and Hidatsa for corn and other agricultural products. East of the Santee lived the Sac, Fox, and Ojibwa. Relations between the Santee and their eastern neighbors were often hostile because of competition for the same resources.

The arrival of Europeans on the shores of North America in the 16th century set in motion fundamental changes in native societies. The first affected were, of course, those who lived along the Atlantic coast and in nearby inland areas. As European settlements encroached on traditional native territories, conflicts arose.

As a result of European expansion and increased warfare, Native Americans in eastern North America saw their lands diminished in size and their lives changed forever. Some people continued to reside on a small portion of their original homeland. Many others left the area, hoping to find peace and prosperity further to the west. However, because these lands were occupied by other native nations, the westward movement of some groups caused the displacement and relocation of others. And as whites pushed further west, pressures to displace native peoples intensified.

These events affected the Santee early in the 18th century. By that time, Santees living in Manitoba and Saskatchewan abandoned the region because of increasing conflict with Ojibwas and Crees coming from the east. The Santees could not adequately defend themselves against their well-armed enemies, who obtained guns through trade with British and French merchants, and so were forced to abandon the area and join others of their people in Minnesota. As native peoples entered Santee territory in Minnesota, conflicts occasionally erupted over land and resources. However, greater dangers to Santee life and land came from the invasion of their home-land by American settlers, whose presence began to destabilize the native population by the early 19th century. The Santee responded to the intruders in several ways. Some people confronted the threat to their security with armed resistance. Others accommodated the settlers by agreeing to cede some of their land to the U.S. government in exchange for promises of protection— promises that the government soon ignored. And other Santees left the region, hoping to find peace and security farther to the west in the United States or to the north in the woods and prairies of central Canada.

None of the Santee's strategies led to lasting stability. Those people who resisted were attacked and ultimately defeated by the American military. Those who ceded part of their territory to the government were repeatedly pressured into selling more land until little, if any, remained in their possession. And those Santees who withdrew to other regions eventually faced the expansion of American and Canadian settlements and saw their land surrounded and diminished.

Despite the numerous hardships endured by the Santee in the 19th century, they have survived on the lands that they now control and have rebuilt their communities, incorporating changes wrought by new ways of living while keeping some of their distinctive values and traditions. ▲

Dakota men spear fish through holes cut in the ice of a frozen river. Santee women were responsible for agriculture, men for hunting and fishing.

2

SANTEE
TRADITIONS

The Santee maintained their traditional culture in the woodlands and mountains of Minnesota until the middle of the 19th century. Their ways of living were well suited to their rich, varied environment. Abundant natural resources and fertile land supplied the people with food and raw materials.

The four bands of the Santee Dakota each had their own territory concentrated from east to west across southern and central Minnesota. The people lived in small settlements situated near rivers or lakes. Most villages contained no more than 400 or 500 people, and many contained far fewer. The Santee did not reside in the same villages all year. Instead, they followed a yearly cycle of settlement relocations, moving to new sites within their customary territory during different seasons to be close to available supplies of wild grains, fruits, plants, and animals.

The Santee had two different types of housing depending on the season. When settled in permanent villages during the spring and summer months, Santees lived in sturdy wooden houses. The houses were constructed by women, although men helped put up the roofs. House frames were made of elm wood posts set in the ground about a foot or two apart to form a rectangle. The posts supported walls and a roof, all covered with elm bark cut into pieces of five or six square feet. Small houses had a single door, whereas larger dwellings had doors at both the front and back. A wooden platform was built at the entrance for drying foods as well as for sleeping when summer nights were hot.

The Santee built wide benches along the houses' interior walls about two feet above the ground. The benches were used for sitting, sleeping, and storing possessions. A hearth for cooking was set in the center of the house, with an opening in the roof above it so that smoke from the fire could escape.

The size of wooden houses varied, but most accommodated at least 25 people. Residents were usually related, although patterns of relationship varied. Some domestic units were based on ties among male kin, others among female kin. Households typically consisted of several families, including an elder couple, their sons or daughters, and the families of some of their married children.

The Santee's second type of housing was used when people traveled to small, temporary settlements during the fall and winter. They then lived in tipis, cone-shaped dwellings made from buffalo hides and wood. Tipis were round at their base and tapered to a smoke hole at the top. They accommodated one or perhaps two families.

In order to construct a tipi, Santee women trimmed 10 or 12 buffalo hides and sewed them together. The hides were fitted over a frame of wooden poles made by the men. Two additional hides were draped over the smoke hole at the top. These hides served as flaps and were opened to allow smoke to escape from a cooking fire or to let in sunlight and air. The flaps were closed to keep out rain or snow. The doorway of a tipi was covered with an extra buffalo hide that could be opened or closed. Tipis were secured to the ground with stones or wooden pegs spaced around the perimeter. In warm weather, the bottom of the tipi was rolled up to permit fresh air to circulate. In cold weather, women made flooring out of dried swamp grass and also packed the grass against the inside of the tipi for insulation.

Tipis were particularly well suited to the Santee's lifestyle. Once their basic components had been constructed, these lightweight structures were easy to assemble, take apart, transport, and reassemble.

Inside their houses and tipis, Santees arranged buffalo-hide bedding and seating for added comfort. These furnishings, as well as the dwellings themselves, were the property of the women residents. The Santee's personal possessions included clothing, ornaments, containers of various sizes and shapes, wooden dishes and spoons, cooking utensils, hunting equipment, and tools such as knives, scrapers, and hatchets.

Santee clothing was made from animal hides. Women wore deerskin skirts, blouses, and dresses. In cold weather, they wore deerskin leggings that reached from the knee to the ankle. Men wore breechcloths and shirts of deerskin. Their leggings covered the entire leg. When working outdoors in cold weather, men wore two sets of leggings. Men and women wore moccasins of deerskin or buffalo hide to protect their feet. In winter, they covered themselves with buffalo robes with the hair side turned inward.

Santee men and women wore their hair in distinctive styles. Men cut their

This drawing depicts the two primary types of Santee Sioux dwelling. In the foreground is the tipi, which provided temporary shelter to one or two families when the tribe was on the move or in their temporary fall and winter villages. In the background are the larger wood-frame habitations that were home to as many as 25 or 30 people in the Santees' permanent villages.

hair in front across the forehead and wore the remainder long and loose. Women wore their hair in two braids. Both sexes adorned themselves and their clothing with paints and ornaments. Young women painted a small red spot at the top of their head where their hair was parted and sometimes added red spots on each cheek. Young men painted more elaborate markings on their faces with pigments of various colors. On special occasions, Santees wore necklaces and bracelets made of shells, beads, and animal bones or teeth. They decorated their clothing with beadwork embroidery, shells, and painted designs.

The Santee transported their clothing, utensils, and tools to new settlements by dog-pulled *travois*. A travois consisted of two shafts of wood that were attached to the sides of the animal and allowed to trail behind on the ground. Clothing and bedding were piled on the poles, and small utensils, tools, or ornaments were placed in a basket that was suspended between the poles. Babies or young children were sometimes carried in the baskets as well.

The Santees breaking camp, as depicted by the American artist Seth Eastman. The travois (behind horse at center left) was commonly used by the Santee to transport goods.

Once settled in their villages, Santees engaged in numerous subsistence activities, including hunting, fishing, gathering wild foods, and farming. Although men and women generally performed different tasks, their labor was equally valued, and everyone cooperated in a task if the need arose.

Women were responsible for planting and harvesting crops. In springtime, they planted seeds using a digging stick, a long wooden pole with a sharpened end. Corn, the Santee's major crop, was planted deep in small, cone-shaped mounds after the corn seeds had been soaked until they sprouted. Some varieties of corn ripened in early summer; others were harvested in the fall. Corn was boiled, roasted, or sun dried and pounded into meal, thus preserving it for later use.

In spite of the Santees' agricultural efforts, wild foods actually constituted a greater portion of their diet. Women gathered plants and other resources from spring until late autumn. In early spring, they tapped maple trees with a single axe stroke and caught the flowing sap in wooden basins. The sap was boiled over fire until it formed a thick syrup and was then poured into small containers to set into a hard sugar.

Huge herds of buffalo migrated across the plains each summer on the westernmost fringes of the Santee territory. The first white visitors to the Sioux country were awed by the richness and variety of animals to be found there.

ship influenced marriage choices because people belonging to the same group were forbidden to marry.

Marriages were often arranged by parents, usually taking into account the wishes of the couple involved. Before marriage, a husband-to-be gave his future wife's family valuable gifts, such as deerskin or buffalo hides, clothing, and ornaments. Acceptance of a man's gifts by the woman and her family constituted an announcement of marriage. A feast was then hosted by the new wife's parents for relatives of both of the spouses.

But couples did not always wait for their parents to arrange a marriage. A man signaled his interest by giving gifts to the woman of his choice. He might appear outside her home in the evening and play love songs on a wooden flute. A woman might find reasons to go outdoors alone when she knew the man she liked was nearby. The two exchanged smiles and brief talk, keeping in mind the Santee's custom of shyness and reserve between unmarried women and men.

Upon marriage, a couple usually resided with the wife's family for a few

While most sugar was made from maple sap, Santee women also tapped birch, ash, and box elder trees. Birch and ash trees yielded a dark, bitter sap that was used as medicine. Box elders produced a white, very sweet sugar that was highly prized. Santees sometimes ate small pieces of sugar as treats or mixed the sugar with wild rice, corn, or dried meat. In any form, sugar was considered a delicacy, and the Santee usually reserved its consumption for special occasions.

In summertime, women harvested rich supplies of wild rice growing in marshy lakes. Working in teams of two, they paddled their birch-bark canoes to the stands of wild rice and hit the plants lightly with a wooden rod so that the rice was loosened and fell into the canoe. Later, the rice was *hulled* and the grain was separated from the chaff. Although most rice was taken back to the villages, some was hidden in holes dug in the ground. People remembered the sites and returned to retrieve the surplus grain when in need.

Santee women collected many other varieties of plants and berries. Blackberries, huckleberries, and cranberries were eaten raw, added to soups, or mixed with dried meat and fat. Whole cherries were pounded into pulp and made into small cakes. In addition to fruits, women gathered wild potatoes, turnips, teepsinna roots, lily roots, wild beans, and acorns. Some plants were eaten raw or added to stews. Others were dried in the sun and kept for future meals.

While women were planting crops and gathering wild foods, Santee men supplied their families with meat from animals, birds, and fish. They took numerous varieties of birds using bows and arrows or snares. Waterfowl such as ducks, geese, loons, and cranes were especially prized, and birds' eggs were collected as well.

Men fished in nearby waterways that teemed with trout, lake sturgeon, and bass. Fishing equipment consisted of spears, bows and arrows, traps of various designs, and fish lines made from hemp or sinew. Santees sometimes dammed up small brooks and drove the fish into large baskets. In winter, they fished through holes cut into the ice of frozen lakes and rivers. When fish came to the opening, they were caught with spears or arrows attached to long strings. Men also hunted deer, elk, bear, moose, and muskrat in the dense woodlands of Santee territory. Santees who lived close to the prairies and plains hunted buffalo as well. Hunting gear consisted of bows and arrows, lances, knives, and hatchets, all made from wood, bone, and stone.

In midsummer, huge herds of buffalo migrated through the prairies near western portions of Santee territory. At that time, some families left their villages, set up camps on the prairies, and organized *communal* hunting expeditions. During the period of buffalo hunting, all hunters were expected to follow strict rules. For example, it was crucial that no man start out on his own because a single mistake could frighten away thousands of buffalo, resulting in the loss of meat and hides for the entire Santee community. After the rules were publicly announced by *heralds*, a group of men known as the soldiers' lodge, distinguished for their skill in hunting and warfare, functioned as a village police force. If any man violated the rules, the soldiers' lodge meted out swift punishment. They approached the guilty man's tipi, called out all the residents, and immediately cut the tipi to shreds with knives and hatchets and destroyed all of the wrongdoer's personal possessions.

Once hunting began, Santees used blinds made of brush to conceal their presence as they neared a herd. When all hunters were in position, a signal was given, and the buffalo were attacked with bows and arrows or lances. In this manner many animals were killed during the hunting season. Some of the meat was cooked and eaten fresh, but the majority was dried and preserved in the form of *pemmican*, dried meat pounded into a powder and mixed with fat and berries.

In autumn, men hunted deer, which were abundant in nearby woods. At that time, Santees usually left their summer villages and dispersed into the forests in small groups of related families. Hunters' activities were coordinated by a council of experienced men. The council made decisions concerning the directions that hunters should take in their daily expeditions as well as the relocation of camps when an area of

several square miles had been hunted over. Each day before sunrise, men left the camp in small groups and fanned out over a large area. They used bows and arrows or lances and also set traps along paths in the woods. In the evening, when the day's first successful hunter returned to camp with a deer, his name was announced to all by a village herald. Hearing his name called out was an honor to the hunter as well as a source of pride for his whole family.

Men in a hunting group divided deer meat according to established customs, giving each hunter a specific portion. The hunter who killed the animal kept the skin in addition to his portion of the meat.

During winter, Santee men caught muskrats and beavers in brooks, small rivers, and lakes. After locating animals' lodges, they dismantled them with spears, easily catching the animals within.

Santee families were united by strong bonds of kinship, loyalty, affection, and mutual obligations. The Santee had a system of relationship based on social units called *clans*, each one named after an animal or bird. A clan is a group of people who claim relationship with one another. Since a clan may contain hundreds of people, individuals cannot trace their actual relationship to every member of the group, but they believe they are related. Santees belonged to clans on the basis of descent through women. Therefore, children were automatically members of their mother's group. Clan member-

The Santee engage in a spirited game of lacrosse. Numerous native peoples across the continent played some variation of the sport, which they believed had been given them by the Creator for their enjoyment.

years. Once their union was well established, a couple might either move with the husband's kin or remain with the wife's family. Strict rules of respectful behavior were followed by parents and their children's spouses. Parents-in-law and their sons- and daughters-in-law avoided speaking to or looking directly at one another.

Most Santee marriages involved the union of one man and one woman. However, some households consisted of a man married to two or more women. In these cases, the women were usually sisters. *Polygamy*, or plural marriages, may have been more common in times

of warfare, when the ratio of men to women declined.

Husbands and wives were expected to treat each other with respect and cooperate in their household tasks. But if a couple became unhappy or quarreled frequently, they were free to separate and seek other mates.

Santee families hoped for the birth of many children. Parents treated their children with kindness and great affection. Adults taught children proper behavior by setting good examples and giving gentle encouragement.

Children received names according to their gender and birth order. The

Santee had a stock of 10 names, 5 for girls and 5 for boys. A first-born girl was called Winona; a first boy, Chaska. Each of the other eight names was given in a set order to subsequent children. Santees used these birth-order names for a relatively short time, since children were soon given additional names. New names possibly referred to a physical or personality trait or to a meaningful event in the child's life. Young men, especially those who performed heroic deeds, were sometimes granted the name of a respected ancestor.

Young children spent much of their time in play with their peers. They had many games that taught them skills and gave them endurance and strength. As children matured, their play prepared them for adult life. Boys had toy bows and arrows that they used to acquire skills they would need as hunters. Girls learned their future roles by helping their mothers collect wild plants, prepare meals, and care for younger siblings.

Community and personal bonds among the Santee were strengthened through exchanges of goods and gifts. Families shared their resources with great generosity. Women gave food to people in their community who were sick or unable to support themselves. The families of unsuccessful hunters received shares of meat brought in by other men. And travelers were treated with hospitality and offered food and shelter.

Santees gave gifts of tools, ornaments, and dogs to people they liked.

In time, recipients of such presents reciprocated, thus establishing and reinforcing mutual social and emotional bonds. In some cases, two people entered into a more formalized friendship. Two men or two women proclaimed their friendship, exchanged gifts, and pledged to help each other in times of need.

Most Santees acted in a fashion considered appropriate by their community, but people who committed offenses against others were subjected to teasing, public ridicule, and open criticism. Such treatment usually led wrongdoers to change their behavior. Serious offenses, such as assault or murder, were rare. When they occurred, individuals who committed violent acts sought to atone by giving valuable presents to the victim or his or her family. If the gifts were accepted, a reconciliation with the offender was achieved. However, in cases of homicide, a victim's family might seek revenge by assaulting or killing the murderer or one of his or her relatives.

Leadership in Santee communities depended on family ties, personality, intelligence, and acquired skills. Each Santee band had a leader, or chief, whose position usually passed from father to eldest son, although such inheritance was by no means automatic. Conflicts sometimes arose between brothers who claimed rights to inherit or other relatives who wished to succeed a deceased chief. The position of chief was associated with varying degrees of influence, depending on the qualities of the man himself. If a chief was intelligent, generous, well spoken, and successful in hunting or warfare, his opinions were taken seriously and his advice usually heeded. However, if he lacked wisdom, was quick to judgment, or behaved improperly, he had little, if any, influence in his community. In such cases, the advice of others was sought.

Oratory, which was esteemed as an art, was an important attribute of a chief or of any other influential Santee. A leader's effectiveness was often a direct result of his speaking skills, and chiefs often sought to persuade others with forceful, eloquent speeches.

Matters that affected the entire community were discussed and decided in meetings called by a council of village elders. All men and women could attend and voice their opinions. The Santee's system of government was described by Samuel Pond, a Congregational minister living among the Santee in the middle of the 19th century:

> The government of the Dakotas was purely democratic, the people holding all the powers of government in their own hands, and never delegating them to others except temporarily and for a special purpose. They claimed and exercised the right of deciding all questions which concerned the public interest. Their decisions were made in councils, frequently after long and animated debates, and sometimes not until after several successive meetings.

The decision was according to the will of the majority; but they seldom, if ever, attempted to carry out a measure when the parties for and against it were nearly equal in numbers. If, when a measure was proposed in council, there was a general response of "Yes," the ayes had it and the measure was adopted; but if there was a general silence or a feeble response, it was lost.

Chiefs were mainly concerned with matters of peace, security in their communities, trade, and relations with outsiders. Leadership in war was the domain of other men. War chiefs were skilled warriors who were responsible for defending their settlements and organizing military expeditions against enemies. Warfare was carried out by small groups of men who joined together after hearing the leader's plans and tactics. Participation was completely voluntary. If a man thought well of the objectives and plans, he might join, but if he thought the campaign ill-advised he could choose not to go.

Santee warriors used bows and arrows, spears, clubs, and hatchets and carried shields made of buffalo hides. Once they entered enemy territory, they did not hunt animals or light fires in order to lessen their chances of being detected. Santee warriors preferred to ambush an unsuspecting enemy in the woods or descend upon a rival village at daybreak. In traditional warfare, Santees did not aim to annihilate an entire group but rather to injure or kill a few enemies to exact revenge for previous attacks against the Santee. When they had to defend their own settlements, warriors dug trenches and awaited their foes. Women, children, and older men hid in deep pits dug into the ground.

Warfare contained a ritual component in the calculation of military honors. Like other native peoples in the Midwest and West, Santees ranked war exploits in a set order. The most honorable action was to strike or kill an enemy at close range with a club or hatchet. Such an exploit demonstrated a warrior's bravery, daring, and quickness. To the Santee, shooting an enemy from a distance displayed neither skill nor bravery. Men who performed the most honored deeds were highly praised when they returned to their communities. They were thereafter entitled to wear eagle feathers in their hair as public symbols of their valor.

The Santee's traditional customs and ways of living enabled them to make use of the land and its resources. Men and women provided themselves and their families with food, clothing, tools, and shelter. Their adaptation to the world around them, and their ability to survive and prosper in that world, was summed up by Samuel Pond in 1834:

> While the Dakotas follow the occupations of their ancestors, they have use for all those instincts and habits which they derive from them. That hardihood of body and stoical fortitude of mind, which enable them to encounter hardships with resolution and endure suffering without repining, that watchfulness never remitted, that self-possession which never deserts them, that habit of observation which nothing can escape, and that sagacity or instinct that enables them to find their way, without chart or compass, through an unknown region,—all these things, and many more like them, are their inheritance.▲

At top is a pair of Santee moccasins, made of moose and caribou hide, porcupine quills, leather cording, and thread. At bottom is a patterned deerskin upper for a moccasin yet to be stitched.

Sioux men dance the Bear Dance. The Santee believed that spirits inhabited all beings and certain objects in the world, and that all living things and some seemingly inanimate objects possessed a soul. The bear was a being of special power and as such was accorded particular veneration.

3

THE "GREAT MYSTERY"

The religion of the Santee centered on beliefs in spirit powers existing in many forms. Spirit powers, called *Takuwakan*, or the "Great Mystery," were invisible essences but could be embodied in various shapes. The Santee believed that some spirit powers had the shape of animals or birds, and others had the shape of humans. Still others were forms or forces of nature, such as Earth, Sun, Moon, Thunder, and Lightning. Plants and trees also had spirit powers, and certain stones and other inanimate objects could contain supernatural force as well. "The elements and majestic forces in nature, Lightning, Wind, Water, Fire, and Frost," the Santee writer Charles Eastman explained, "were regarded with awe as spiritual powers. We believed that the spirit pervades all creation and that every creature possesses a soul. The tree, the waterfall, the grizzly bear, each is an embodied Force, and as such an object of reverence."

Spirit powers, in whatever shape, influenced the course of human lives. They brought health, good fortune, and success in one's endeavors. And they protected people from harm. Spirit powers also caused illness, death, and calamity. Santees tried to acquire as much knowledge as they could about the supernatural realm in order to make positive use of spirit powers and protect themselves from potential harm.

Most spirit powers were neither always kind nor always malevolent. They could help people or hurt them depending, in part, on the way people behaved toward them. But spirits did not act only in response to people's deeds. They had strong wills and desires of their own and did as they pleased. And, of course, they had knowledge and abilities far superior to those of ordinary people.

Some supernatural beings behaved in ways considered unusual or unpredictable by human standards. One being, called Heyoka, did everything in reverse of the normal pattern. He said yes when he meant no, walked backward, and felt cold in summer and hot in winter. Another spirit, called Unktomi, or Spider, was a trickster: mischievous and untrustworthy yet also charming and witty. Unktomi often caused trouble for others and got into trouble himself, but he always managed to survive. Santees believed that certain stones had spirit essences and could act in extraordinary ways as well. Sacred stones demonstrated their power by their ability to move. They could roll on the ground at will, leaving a track behind them.

Animals were thought to have a great deal of supernatural power. Each species had its spirit protector. If hunters showed respect for animals, the protectors responded by allowing the animals to be caught. If protector spirits thought they had been slighted, hunters' efforts would fail. Men therefore prayed to animal spirits when setting out on hunting expeditions and later thanked the spirits if they were successful. A thanksgiving ritual in honor of a bear killed by a Santee hunter was described by Father Louis Hennepin, a French priest who visited the Indians in 1680:

> The hunters' faces and bodies were smeared with paint, each man being painted with the symbol of some animal appropriate to his family or selected by his own fancy. Some had their hair short, full of bear grease, and decorated with red and white feathers. Others sprinkled their heads with the down of birds, which clung to the grease. They all danced with their hands on their hips, striking the soles of their feet upon the ground so hard that they left foot-prints.

Much of Santee religious practice consisted of individual prayers to spirits. In their prayers, people asked for guidance, knowledge, protection, good health, and recovery from illness. They prayed for their own success and for the well-being of the entire community.

The Santee demonstrated their sincerity and willingness to make sacrifices by fasting and by giving spirits offerings of food, tobacco, and valuable objects such as clothing, ornaments, tools, and animal skins. They placed the objects on the ground or on stones, threw them into the water, or suspended them from trees.

Santees prepared themselves for important or dangerous endeavors by undergoing ritual purification in sweat baths. Through sweats, people cleansed their bodies and minds so that they would be ready to participate in rituals and receive messages or visions from the supernatural world. Sweats were conducted in small huts or *sweat lodges* that could accommodate several people. Steam was produced by pouring water over heated stones placed in the lodge. Bundles of cedar bark provided a fragrant incense that was thought to be pleasing to spirit beings.

The Santee believed that people could have direct contact with spirit beings through dreams while asleep and through visions while awake. During sleep, spirits sometimes came to people, imparted messages from the supernatural realm, and gave instructions concerning dreamers' actions and warnings about future events. They taught dreamers songs and prayers to use when calling on them in times of need.

Contact with spirits also occurred in visions. In some cases, a spirit appeared spontaneously to an individual, perhaps while she or he was gathering fruit or hunting alone in the forest, walking silently along a riverbank, or passing through an area protected by a particular spirit. In other cases, an individual actively sought contact with spirits in order to acquire knowledge, ensure success, or be protected from harm. Although all Santees could have direct contact with the supernatural realm, some women and men obtained special powers. Through revelations from spirits, they could foretell future events and interpret dreams and omens.

In addition to private prayers, offerings, and contacts with the supernatural realm, Santees conducted public ceremonial feasts to honor spirit beings and to thank them for successful hunting or war expeditions, good harvests of corn or wild rice, and recovery from illness. Feasts were accompanied by generous gifts to those in attendance.

The Santee performed a variety of sacred dances dedicated to animal spir-

In wintertime, the Sioux placed the corpses of their dead in the branches of trees, where they would be safe from scavenging animals.

its, such as Bear and Elk, or to forces of nature, such as Thunder and Sun. Dances also followed war victories and formed part of other ceremonial and social occasions.

Santee religion stressed the role of spirit forces in maintaining good health or recovering from illness. Like peoples throughout the world, Santees had a complex theory of disease causation and treatment. Their medical practitioners were skilled in practical and ritual methods of diagnosis and treatment. Healers, both men and women, were trained by established practitioners who knew medicinal qualities of many varieties of plants, tree barks, and animal and fish oils. Some natural substances were applied externally as salves; others were made into teas and ingested by patients. Healers treated wounds, set broken bones, and massaged sore or injured muscles.

Since Santees believed that many ailments were caused by spirit forces, healers did not rely solely on their practical skills. They also used spiritual powers and ritual treatments consisting of prayers, songs, dances, and certain specific acts believed effective for particular diseases. Through prayers, fasting, and visions, healers received the power to cure from spirit helpers who revealed the cause of a patient's illness and directed the healer to proper treatments.

In the Santee belief system, the many possible supernatural reasons for disease included the intrusion of a foreign object into a patient's body. In these cases, healers extracted the harmful object by sucking on the patient's body at the place where the object had made its entry, usually an arm or shoul-

Sioux burial scaffolds. The Santee believed that the souls of the deceased journeyed to the land of the spirits along a pathway formed by the stars.

der. Objects such as small pebbles or feathers or *amorphous* substances were often found to be the responsible agents. Healers drew out the disease-causing object, spit it into a dish, and threw it away, thereby eliminating its harmful effects.

Some Santee healers belonged to a prestigious organization called the Medicine Society or Medicine Lodge. In some cases, people joined after actively seeking membership; others were chosen by the group without having demonstrated prior interest. New members learned medicinal and spiritual cures during a ritual of initiation, one of the most sacred of all Santee ceremonies. Each initiate had a sponsor, usually a relative, who was already a member of the society. Sponsors gave novices medicine bags made of animal skin that contained objects having spiritual healing powers, such as stones, feathers, and animal bones.

The rite of initiation, or Medicine Dance, was held in a Medicine Lodge built in a clearing in the woods. Private ceremonies were held in the lodge for several days preceding the main dance. During these rituals, initiates learned prayers and songs and were taught the proper behavior of Medicine Society members.

The Medicine Dance itself was a public ceremony, observed by the entire community as well as by people living in nearby settlements. It began in the early morning when initiates and members arranged themselves in two rows, one on each side of the Medicine Lodge.

Dancers faced the center, holding their powerful medicine bags, and sang songs accompanied by constant drumming. The dramatic conclusion of one performance of a Medicine Dance was described by Charles Eastman:

> The initiates were led out in front of the Lodge and placed in a kneeling position upon a carpet of rich robes and furs, the men upon the right hand, stripped and painted black, with a round spot of red just over the heart, while the women, dressed in their best, were arranged upon the left. Both sexes wore the hair loose, as if in mourning or expectation of death. An equal number of Society members, each appointed to one of the novices, faced them at a distance of perhaps fifty feet.
>
> The members assumed an attitude of dignity, crouching slightly, and grasping their medicine bags in both hands. Swinging their arms forward at the same moment, they uttered a cry in perfect unison, with startling effect. In the midst of a breathless silence, they stepped foward, ending a yard or so from the row of kneeling victims, with a mighty swing of the sacred bags that would seem to project all their mystic power into the bodies of the initiates. Instantly, the initiates all fell forward, apparently lifeless.

After being "shot" with spirit power, the fallen initiates were covered with buffalo robes as though they were to be buried. A short time later, they were resurrected by songs and prayers recited by Medicine Society members.

Initiates regained consciousness and each coughed up a small shell or pebble. Once they returned to life, novices joined the members in dancing and singing until nightfall. Afterward, a public feast was held for all participants in the Medicine Society as well as for spectators in attendance.

Santee religion included ceremonies conducted by families to mark significant events in their lives. Birth, naming, and death were accompanied by ritual activities and feasts. Pregnant women observed a number of ritual rules to protect their children from harm and ensure a good future. They did not eat meat and avoided contact with animals lest spirit powers adversely affect their baby's health. Expectant mothers focused their thoughts on their baby's character, choosing a well-respected ancestor as a model for their child. Santees believed that a mother's mental activities during pregnancy affected her child's personality and its physical and spiritual growth.

Mothers' influence on their babies' spiritual development continued after birth and was deemed especially strong during the first two years of life. Mothers were expected to set good examples by reciting prayers to protect and instruct their children. They taught their sons and daughters about the powers of the Great Mystery and the necessity of honoring the spirit world.

Shortly after a baby was born, a herald announced the news throughout the settlement. The child was soon given her or his personal name in a ceremony sponsored by the parents and conducted by elder men who had excellent reputations in the community. Some names gave spirit protections to their bearers. Santee children learned to pray to spirit beings and to show their humility by making offerings of valued possessions. Young children offered small ornaments or toys to the supernatural world. They sometimes sacrificed dogs that they kept as favorite pets.

As children grew up, they gradually prepared to make contact with the spirit realm. They fasted occasionally in order to acquire physical and spiritual strength. Then, when they reached their middle or late teens, they were encouraged to engage in solitary *vision quests* for spirit powers and protections. Although young men and young women might both seek visions, young men were more likely to do so. A vision seeker began by undergoing ritual purification in a sweat lodge. Afterward, he or she set out at sunrise and ventured into the woods or onto the prairies. Standing alone, the seeker recited prayers and sang songs that honored supernatural beings and forces. While fasting and staying awake for several days, the seeker hoped to be visited by a spirit being. If the seeker was successful, a spirit appeared and gave him or her instructions or revealed special knowledge. The spirit taught the seeker songs to use as protection and as a means of calling on the spirit's aid.

When seekers returned to their settlements, they again entered a sweat lodge for a purifying bath. Thereafter, they thought often about their visions and sang their sacred songs when in distress or danger. People did not tell others the nature of their visions because they regarded the vision as a private experience with intense spiritual meaning.

The last of life's moments was marked with solemn rituals by the Santee. When someone died, his or her body was dressed in fine clothing and wrapped in buffalo robes. The body was buried within a few days unless the ground was frozen. In that case, the body was placed on a scaffold secured high in a tree and buried later when the ground thawed. As a reminder of the deceased's spiritual presence, a lock of her or his hair was cut and wrapped in beautiful clothing. Called a spirit bundle, it was kept by the deceased's spouse or parents and suspended from a pole in their house.

The Santee believed that people had immortal souls. After death, the soul separated from the body and eventually made its way to the land of spirits by following the path of spirits formed by stars in the sky. In the land of spirits, souls existed as they had during life. Since Santees thought that life in the afterworld was similar to life on earth, mourners buried small objects of clothing, ornaments, tools, or utensils with the deceased, believing that souls used these objects in the afterworld.

Santees expressed grief over the death of a relative or friend by wailing and lamenting their loss. They sang or chanted sorrowful songs and called out for the deceased. Close relatives kept long periods of mourning. Women showed their grief for a deceased husband or child by cutting their hair short, giving away their valued clothing, and making gashes in their legs with a sharp piece of flint. Men painted their faces black and made cuts in their arms after the death of their wives. Surviving spouses wore shabby clothing, said little, and sought solitude. They sat at their mates' graves for many hours during many days, either in silent thought or loud lamenting. Parents showed similar signs of mourning at the death of their children.

The period of mourning ended after approximately one year. At that time, relatives held a public feast to honor the deceased. His or her possessions were given away to relatives and community members, and the lock of hair that had been cut from the body was finally buried.

The Santees' religion provided the people with explanations for life and death, gave them courage to face adversity, and encouraged them to express happiness in their successes. The people's lives were filled with occasions to seek guidance and aid from the supernatural world and to thank spirits for their protection. As Charles Eastman wrote, "Every act of life is, in a very real sense, a religious act. The Santee recognize the spirit in all creation, and believe that they draw from it spiritual power." ▲

Representatives of the U.S. government and delegates of the Santee Sioux meet at Traverse des Sioux in 1849 to conclude a treaty whereby the United States would acquire all the Santee territory in Minnesota and South Dakota.

STRANGERS IN THEIR MIDST

For hundreds of years, the Santee lived in prosperity in what is now the upper Midwest of the United States. They adapted to their environment and adjusted to the presence of other Native Americans who inhabited nearby lands. But in the late 17th century, Europeans arrived in their territory. At first, the foreigners were of little consequence because of their relatively small numbers, but within two centuries, European and American intruders caused disaster for the Santee.

When Santees first met French explorers and traders in 1660, they greeted them with the same hospitality shown to all travelers. Because the party of Frenchmen, led by Paul Radisson and Medard Chouart des Groseilliers, were starving after a long winter in the woods, Santees gave them ample quantities of rice, corn, and meat. Radisson and des Groseilliers had been sent by French merchant companies to explore lands west of the Great Lakes and establish trading networks with native peoples. The French wanted to obtain furs from beavers and muskrats hunted by the Indians. The furs would be sent to Europe to be made into hats and collars that were the rage of fashion throughout the Continent. For their part, Santees welcomed the strangers because they wanted to acquire European tools, utensils, weapons, and cloth. They especially prized metal goods such as kettles, knives, hatchets, scissors, and nails because these items were less likely to break or wear out than traditional gear made from stone, wood, and bone. In addition, men sought guns and ammunition for hunting, while women wanted heavy woolen cloth that they could make into warm robes, coats, and leggings.

When Radisson and des Groseilliers returned to Montreal, then the center of French activity in eastern Canada, they reported the favorable reception given them by the Indians and the pledges of friendship made between the Santee and French nations. Pleased with the reports, French officials sent additional expeditions to strengthen alliances with the native people. And Catholic priests made plans to begin missionary work among the Indians. The first, Father Claude Allouez, traveled to Santee lands in 1665 and noted their prosperous economy and comfortable living conditions.

Visits to Santee settlements by French traders, soldiers, and missionaries increased in the following years. In 1686, Nicholas Perrot, a trader and military officer, built a fort in the midst of Santee territory and shortly thereafter declared the entire region to be under the rule of the French crown. A second fort was established nearby in 1695. In the same year, Pierre Le Sueur invited a Santee leader named Tioscate to Montreal to meet with French officials. Tioscate was well received in Montreal, but before he could return to his people he fell gravely ill and died.

Le Sueur journeyed again to Santee territory in 1700 and built another fort there. The French constructed forts in the region not to threaten the native population but to protect France's economic and military interests against its rival, Great Britain. Recognizing the enormous profits that could be made from the trade in beaver fur, the two European powers each sought to enlarge their trading networks with native peoples. In addition, both nations wanted to expand the territory they controlled in North America.

The competition led France and Great Britain to establish trading and military alliances with native peoples. Each country then tried to create a monopoly by persuading its allies not to trade with its rival. As hostilities between the French and British increased, Indians often came into conflict among themselves. Intertribal warfare intensified, embroiling the Santee in raids with the Ojibwa, Ottawa, Fox, and Sac who lived in present-day Wisconsin, Minnesota, and Illinois. As a result of frequent raids by all sides, Santees gradually left their territory in eastern Minnesota and relocated to the south and west near the Minnesota and Mississippi rivers.

The power struggle between Great Britain and France erupted in armed conflict in 1756. Known as the French and Indian War (1756–63), it was fought between the two European powers and their Indian allies in the Northeast and Midwest. Although the Santee did not participate in the war, they were affected by its outcome. Shortly after Great Britain emerged victorious, British merchants arrived in Santee territory and took over the lucrative trading networks established by the French. Among the first was Jonathan Carver, who visited Santee villages in 1766, followed in 1773 by Peter Pond.

At the same time that the British were expanding trade in the Midwest, they were faced with increased unrest among their colonists in the East. When

Sioux skirmish with white settlers along the upper Mississippi River in July 1848. The next year, Minnesota became an official territory of the United States. Over the next decade the estimated population of 6,000 whites in the territory would increase more than 20-fold, creating an enormous demand for land.

the American Revolution broke out in 1775, British loyalists and American rebels both hoped to win support from the powerful Santee and other native peoples. Failing that, the warring parties hoped that the Indians would at least remain neutral.

In fact, most Santees did remain neutral. Some, however, sided with the British for several reasons. First, they generally had positive relations with British traders and officials. And second, the Santee knew that the government in Great Britain had enacted laws forbidding colonial expansion west of the Appalachian Mountains. Since these restrictions were ignored by colonists

and a steady stream of intruders had been arriving near Santee territory, the Indians distrusted Americans' future intentions.

The British won a strong ally when Wabasha, a Mdewakanton chief, decided to support Britain's cause. Given the rank of general, Wabasha led hundreds of Santee men in attacks against rebel outposts along the Mississippi River. A British official named Patrick Sinclair praised Wabasha and the military skills of the Santee, whom he described as "a warlike people undebauched, under the authority of a chief named Wabasha of very singular and uncommon abilities, who can raise 200 men with ease, accus-

Fort Snelling, here sketched by Seth Eastman in 1848, was located at the source of the Minnesota River, at its confluence with the mighty Mississippi. It thus commanded the reservation the Santee Sioux were made to accept by virtue of the treaties of Traverse des Sioux and Mendota, which stretched in a 10-mile-wide strip for approximately 150 miles along the south side of the Mississippi River.

tomed to all the attention and obedience required by discipline."

Although Sinclair probably overstated Wabasha's control, his statement reflected the high opinion that the British had of Santee warriors and their leaders. Another officer, Charles Phillips, commented, "General Wabasha was well contented with his commission and his warriors are nothing inferior to regular troops."

Even though Great Britain lost the war, relations between Santees and British traders continued. Natives regularly visited British in nearby Canada and exchanged beaver furs for European goods. By the end of the 18th century, Santees had replaced many traditional tools, utensils, and weapons with European manufactures, including brass kettles, woolen cloth and blankets, and iron knives, nails, arrowheads, and hatchets.

It was not until the early years of the 19th century that Santees had their first official contacts with the new American

government. In 1805, they were visited by Lieutenant Zebulon Pike, who had been assigned the task of securing American sovereignty over the vast territory of the so-called Northwest, territory inhabited by many native peoples, including the Santee. Pike was directed to obtain land from Indians so that the government could build forts and trading posts in the region. Seven Santee leaders, all members of the Mdewakanton band, met in council with Pike and discussed his proposals for a treaty to be signed by the Santee and American nations. Pike asked the leaders to cede approximately 100,000 acres of land near the Minnesota, Mississippi, and St. Croix rivers. The treaty did not mention a specific sum as compensation for the territory, but Pike assured the leaders that the land was worth at least $200,000. Of the seven Santees in attendance, only two agreed to the sale. Despite the lack of support from the other five leaders, and despite the fact that the men present represented only one of the four Santee bands, the American government insisted that the treaty was valid. The Senate ratified the document and awarded the Santee a total of $2,000 for their land, a sum that the natives did not receive until 1819.

Although Pike was successful in acquiring land from the Santee, he was unable to obtain the people's loyalty. The fact that Santees continued to trade with British merchants angered American officials. Indeed, trade between Santees and British was steady and lucrative. Pike estimated that Indians brought an annual total of 555 packs of furs to British merchants in exchange for some $32,000 worth of goods.

The Santees' preference for the British was made clear in 1812, when war broke out between Great Britain and the United States. Santees aided the British, as did most other Indians living in the Northwest Territory, because of their close ties to British merchants and their fears of American expansionism. During the war, hundreds of Santee men fought alongside British troops, causing the defeat of Americans at a number of outposts in the region.

When the U.S. government offered to negotiate a peace settlement with Britain in 1814, Lieutenant Colonel McDouall of the British army assured the Santee that "should the King deign to listen to the proposal which the enemy have made for peace, it will be on the express condition that your interests shall be first considered, your just

claims admitted, and no infringement of your rights permitted in [the] future." Despite McDouall's assurances, the Treaty of Ghent, which officially ended the war, acknowledged American sovereignty over the Northwest. The treaty made no mention of the rights of native peoples who inhabited the territory. In an effort to blunt the meaning of the treaty's terms, British officials met with Santee leaders and offered gifts as thanks for their support during the war. Wabasha responded angrily:

> What is this I see before me? A few knives and blankets! Is this all you promised? You told us you would never let fall the hatchet until the Americans were driven beyond the mountains; that our British Father would never make peace without consulting us. Has that come to pass? Will these paltry presents pay for the men we have lost in battle? Will they soothe the feelings of our friends? Will they make good your promises to us?

And Little Crow, a Mdewakanton chief, added:

> After we have fought for you, endured many hardships, lost some of our people, and awakened the vengeance of our powerful neighbors, you make a peace for yourselves and leave us to obtain such terms as we can! You no longer need our services, and offer us these goods as a compensation for having deserted us. But no! We will not take them; we hold them and yourselves in equal contempt!

The American government moved quickly to obtain pledges of peace and friendship from the Santee and soon began building a series of forts in the region. The first, called Fort Snelling, was constructed in 1819 at the mouth of the Minnesota River. Officials wanted to establish a military presence in order to intimidate native people. They also hoped to quell intertribal warfare because American settlers were entering the territory and feared that conflicts among the Indians threatened their own safety.

To further settlers' interests, the government invited a delegation of Santee, Ojibwa, and Menominee leaders to Washington, D.C., in 1824 to discuss a truce among the native peoples. The government hoped to impress the leaders with American power and thereby persuade them to agree to officials' demands. No conclusive agreement was reached, but the following year, a regional intertribal council was held at Prairie du Chien in present-day Wisconsin. It was attended by hundreds of native people, including representatives of the Santee, Ojibwa, Menominee, Winnebago, Sac and Fox, Iowa, Potawatomi, and Ottawa. The Santee delegation was led by Wabasha, Little Crow, and Shakopee. American officials proposed establishing definite boundaries dividing the territories of each native group. The Indians resisted the proposal because such arbitrary divisions violated their concepts of ownership and access to land. These concepts were enunciated at the council by Caramonee, a Winnebago chief:

Wabasha, photographed here in 1860, was among the Santee leaders who bitterly opposed the reservation treaties, fully expecting that whites would not live up to their terms. His skepticism proved justified.

The lands I claim are mine and nations here know it is not only claimed by us but by our brothers the Sacs and Foxes, Menominees, Iowas, Mahas, and Sioux. They have held it in common. It would be difficult to divide it. It belongs as much to one as the other. I did not know that any of my relations had any particular lands. I had thought that the rivers were the common property of all and not used exclusively by any particular nation.

Little Crow would ultimately be demonized by white settlers as a murderous renegade, but among some of his own people he was initially viewed as being too accommodating of white demands for Santee land.

While the U.S. government was supposedly trying to make peace, it was actually creating conditions that would inevitably lead to warfare by allowing explorers, traders, missionaries, and settlers to enter the region and disrupt the Indians' lives. Major Stephen Long led a large expedition to explore the upper Mississippi and Minnesota rivers. He visited several Santee villages and, like others before him, commented on the people's prosperity. Major Long estimated the total number of Santee to be about 5,700, including 2,500 Sissetons, 1,500 Mdewakantons, 900 Wahpetons, and 800 Wahpekutes. These figures undoubtedly reflected declines in population from previous centuries, before Santees had contact with whites.

During the same period, the Columbia Fur Company and the American Fur Company sent traders to contact the Santee and establish posts in their territory. They wanted native men to supply them with beaver and muskrat furs. As the Santee's involvement in the fur trade increased, men spent less time hunting animals for food. The people began to trade with American merchants for food as well as for tools, utensils, and weapons.

In addition, several Protestant churches sent missionaries to convert Santees to their sect of Christianity. Most prominent among them were Samuel Pond, a Congregational minister; Thomas Williamson of the American Board of Commissioners for Foreign Missions; and Stephen Riggs, a Methodist. By 1830, the Santee were visited regularly by numerous missionaries, all of whom set up residences near trading centers and small government outposts that were developing close to Indian villages.

Soon, American settlers were entering Santee territory looking for land to cultivate. It seemed not to matter that Santees already occupied the land and had done so for countless generations. Increased American settlement led to increased apprehension on the part of the native people. They repeatedly urged American officials, traders, and missionaries to protect their rights to land. But instead, the government sought to benefit settlers by persuading or forcing the Santee to cede more territory. Government officials also wanted to convince Indians to abandon their nomadic hunting and gathering lifestyle and settle in fixed locations, becoming farmers in accordance with American practices. Officials justified their plan by claiming that it would improve the Santee's economy and lead them to "civilization." And, the Americans reasoned, if Santees settled permanently on small farms, they would not need their vast ancestral territory.

In 1837, a delegation of 26 Santee representatives was invited to Washington, D.C., to negotiate an intertribal peace treaty with Sac and Fox leaders. When the Sac and Fox delegates did not arrive, the Santees assumed the council had no further objective. But government officials had other plans. They wanted the Santee to sign a treaty ceding all their land east of the Mississippi River as well as islands in the river. In return, the Americans promised to invest a sum of $100,000 and pay the Santee 5 percent interest on the account "annually, forever." Payment would be made in goods and cash. In addition, the government agreed to give the native people an *annuity* in goods amounting to $10,000 for 20 years. The government promised to spend $8,250 each of the 20 years for medicines, farm equipment, and livestock as well as to provide a physician, farm instructors, and blacksmiths. Finally, the treaty allocated $90,000 to pay American traders directly for "just debts" owed them by the Santees. Twenty-one of the native leaders were persuaded to sign the treaty after officials made veiled threats reminding them of the military power and wealth of the growing American nation.

Numerous problems quickly developed in implementing the government's pledges. Annuity goods typically arrived well after their scheduled date, creating hardships for the many Santees who had given up traditional pursuits because of their decreasing land and resource base. When annuity goods finally did arrive, Santees found that they were poor in quality and insufficient in quantity. In the words of one native man, "After the goods leave Washington, the road is very long and some of the boxes get holes in them and their dollars and goods drop out."

Problems also arose when annuity shares were paid in cash. American traders immediately raised prices in their stores and soon acquired all of the Santee's money. And funds supposedly intended to help native people with economic, medical, and educational support were sent to local government agents in charge of overseeing Indian affairs. Since agents were often either incompetent or corrupt, the money was rarely put to uses described in the treaty.

After the Treaty of 1837 was signed, missionaries increased and broadened their activities among the Santee. They built churches in hopes of converting the people to Christianity and boarding schools to educate native children. However, most Santees were not interested in attending missions or sending their children to school. They especially resisted the boarding schools because they did not want children to be separated from their families and thus from traditional activities and beliefs. Santees also objected to missionaries' insistence on mixing religious and secular education. Although by the middle of the 19th century many Santees accepted the fact that it was no longer possible to fully engage in traditional economic pursuits and were willing to learn new skills, they strongly resented attempts to change their religious beliefs and practices.

As Santees tried to adjust to alterations in their lives, the government proceeded to make any return to traditional activities impossible. When the U.S. Senate created Minnesota Territory from the Northwest region in 1849, the

(Continued on page 57)

THE
ART
OF
THE
PLAINS

Colorful embroidery is the hallmark of Plains Indians crafts. Two features of Santee Sioux embroidery are particularly striking: the use of porcupine quills, and intricate glass beadwork.

The American porcupine was native to the northern and eastern woodlands. There, in the 18th century and before, its quills became popular for embellishing clothing and leather articles. Santee women would sort the quills, which were usually three to four inches long. Then they would dye them with vegetable and mineral colors—blues, yellows, greens, whites, and pinks are a trademark of Santee art—and soften them with spittle. Next the quills were flattened and sewn onto a leather surface with a needle. Santee women were extremely skilled at splicing or tying the quills for use in large areas of design; a finished piece will appear to have been done from one long skein.

At the beginning of the 18th century, European traders began introducing small beads of colored glass to the Santee Sioux as gifts or in exchange for skins and furs. These beads, called "pony beads," became an important feature of Santee craft. By the mid-19th century, pony beads had been replaced in popularity by "seed beads," imported from Venice and Czechoslovakia. The smaller size and elongated shape of the seed bead changed beadwork style; pony beads had been used here and there in larger designs, but now allover beadwork, covering entire surfaces, became common.

Although quillwork declined in popularity and is executed only in very few Northern Plains areas today, many spectacular examples of intricate and beautiful beadwork have survived to provide a fascinating look into the creative life of the Santee Sioux.

Santee moccasins with intricate beadwork, circa 1900.

A fringed deerskin jacket with beadwork depictions of rattlesnakes, various birds, and a turtle. The jacket was made for a white man, J. F. Lenger, probably by Nebraska Santee women, circa 1890.

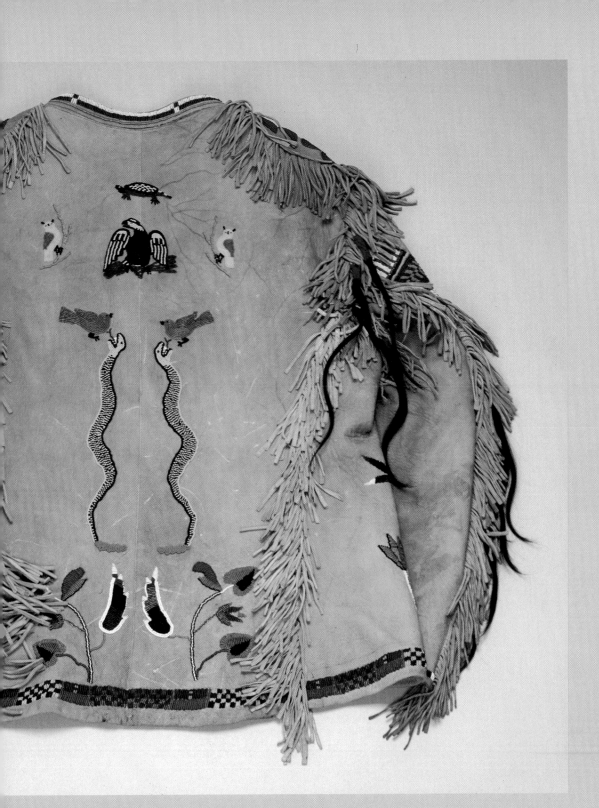

Fringed deerskin pants, also made for J. F. Lenger, circa 1890.

52

Deerskin vest with beadwork design, circa 1900.

A bandolier bag. Worn across one shoulder, it rested on the opposite hip.

54

A pair of leggings, or horse chaps, designed to protect the pants. They were slipped over the pants from the ankle to the knee and were tied with the leather cord.

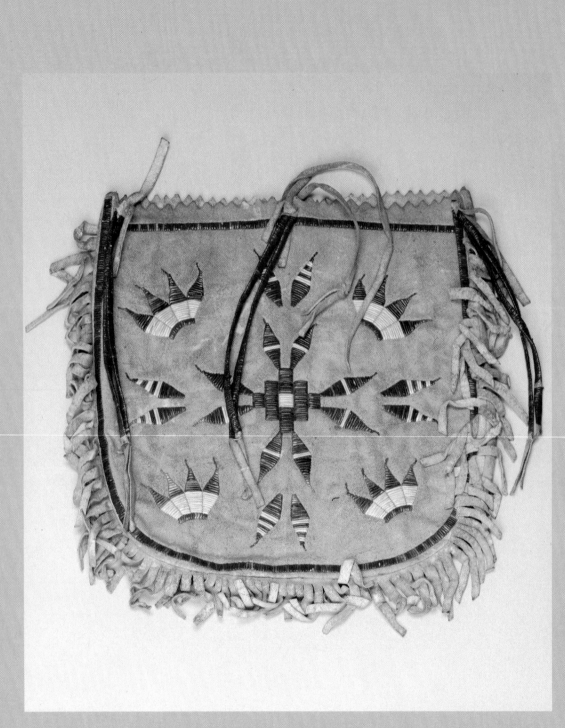

Santee bag with porcupine-quill design, circa 1900. Bright pink was a favorite color in Santee designs.

(Continued from page 48)

newly appointed governor, Alexander Ramsey, immediately began to press the Santee to cede additional territory along the upper Minnesota and Mississippi rivers. Ramsey sought to negotiate two treaties, one with the so-called Upper Sioux, namely the Sisseton and Wahpeton bands, and the other with the Lower Sioux, the Mdewakantons and Wahpekutes. Ramsey and Luke Lea, the commissioner of the Federal Bureau of Indian Affairs, met first with Upper Sioux delegates at Traverse des Sioux and told them that the government wanted to acquire all their land in Minnesota and South Dakota. In exchange for approximately 21 million acres, a small reservation would be set aside for them along the upper Minnesota River. The government promised to invest a sum of $1,360,000 and pay the Santee 5 percent interest annually for 50 years. Another $275,000 was to be paid directly to American traders for debts owed by Santee families. And $30,000 would be used for education and agricultural training. Commissioner Lea told the delegates that other Indian peoples who had sold their land were now "happier and more comfortable, and every year growing better and richer."

Despite Lea's optimistic appraisal, some Santee leaders resisted signing the treaty. One commented, "[Y]ou must think it a great deal of money to give for this land, but you must well understand that the money will all go back to the whites again, and the country will also remain theirs." In the end, Sisseton and Wahpeton leaders agreed to the terms because they felt they had no alternative. Once the document was signed, James Goodhue, the editor of a Minnesota newspaper, wrote, "Thus ended the sale of twenty one millions of acres of the finest land in the world."

Shortly after the Treaty of Traverse des Sioux was concluded, Ramsey and Lea met with leaders of the two Lower Sioux bands at Mendota. Mdewakanton and Wahpekute leaders were even more reluctant to sign than their Upper Sioux counterparts had been. They objected to the dimensions and location of the reservation they would be assigned along the upper Minnesota River, and they commented that the government had failed to deliver money and goods promised in previous treaties. Wabasha, Little Crow, and Wacouta all voiced misgivings, noting that Santees had never benefited from prior agreements with the government. At that point, Lea warned them, "Suppose your Great Father [the president of the United States] wanted your lands and did not want a treaty for your good, he would come with 100,000 men and drive you off to the Rocky Mountains."

Still the chiefs resisted. Wacouta said that his people distrusted the officials' words. "When we were in Washington [in 1837]," he declared, "the chiefs were told many things; which when we came back here, and attempted to carry out, we found could not be done. At the end of three or four years, the Indians found out very different from what they had been told, and all

In the face of never-ending demands for Sioux land, the Santee leader Shakopee, like Little Crow, took up arms against white settlers.

were ashamed." Finally, though, 64 leaders in attendance agreed to sign the treaty. For their land, Mdewakantons and Wahpekutes were to receive 5 percent interest for 50 years on a sum of $1,410,000.

When the treaties of Traverse des Sioux and Mendota were ratified by the U.S. Senate, provisions granting the Santee reservations along the upper Minnesota River were eliminated. Ramsey then met with native leaders and explained that President Franklin Pierce would let them remain on the land "until the whites wanted it." The Indians did not have long to wait. American settlers began arriving in Santee territory even before the treaty had been ratified. They set up farms on Santee land and ordered the Indians to leave. The native people realized that they had once again been betrayed. Wabasha commented, "There is only one thing more which our great father can do, that is, gather us all together on the prairie and surround us with soldiers and shoot us down."

President Pierce finally agreed to let the Santee occupy the lands originally stipulated in the treaties of Traverse des Sioux and Mendota "until the President shall consider it proper to remove them." This statement, imprecise as it was, reassured the Indians for the moment.

By 1854, nearly all the Santee had removed themselves from their traditional homeland to reservations specified in treaties. However, pressure to

Santee Sioux leaders such as Cut Nose, who sat for this photograph in 1862, saw their people betrayed by allies and enemies alike, defeated in battle, cheated out of their land, and finally removed from Minnesota altogether.

leave Minnesota continued, and within a few years this pressure would have catastrophic consequences for the Santee. ▲

Some members of the Santee Sioux delegation that traveled to Washington, D.C., in 1858 to negotiate a new treaty with the U.S. government.

5

THE
DISPOSSESSED

The second half of the 19th century was a momentous period for the Santee. Changes that had begun in earlier years took their toll in lives and property. Among the devastating effects of contact between the native people and foreigners was the spread of diseases originating in Europe but previously unknown in North America. Most serious were smallpox, measles, influenza, and tuberculosis. Because Indians had never been exposed to the organisms that cause these ailments, they had not developed natural resistances or immunities to them. Once the germs were brought to the continent, they spread swiftly and with deadly effect. Countless Indians throughout North America died in epidemics, and the Santee were no exception. In the 1830s, a major smallpox outbreak among them resulted in hundreds of deaths. In the following decade, epidemics of cholera, influenza, and whooping cough killed many more. Additional deadly outbreaks occurred in the 1850s and 1860s.

The Santee's economy suffered during the same period. Most people depended on the fur trade to supply some of their tools, utensils, weapons and cloth, but they had difficulty obtaining these items because their income from the fur trade declined as the number of beavers in their territory dwindled. Although the Santee trapped other animals, beaver furs had always fetched the highest price. For example, hunters received only 10 cents for each muskrat skin, compared with three dollars for each beaver. At the same time that their income declined, Santee hunters were finding it increasingly difficult to supply their families with enough food from the wild because their hunting territories were taken by terms of treaties and by settlers' illegal encroachment. And now they had to compete with Americans for the ever-decreasing number of wild animals still to be found.

Worsening economic conditions forced Santees to become increasingly dependent on annuity goods and cash guaranteed to them in treaties. But annuity shipments and payments were usually late, leading to periods of starvation for many people.

The Santees' economic insecurity was matched by uncertainty about their ability to remain on reservation lands in Minnesota. In accordance with treaties and assurances given by American officials, the Santee resided on several reservations along the Minnesota River north of their original villages. However, local politicians continued to pressure the federal government to evict the Indians from the territory. In 1854, the Mdewakanton chief Little Crow was invited to Washington to meet with President Pierce and Charles Mix, commissioner of Indian Affairs. Although Pierce reassured Little Crow that the Santee could remain on their lands "forever," the chief worried that the Americans' power and the settlers' appetite for land would one day force the Santee to move farther west.

Conditions on reservations steadily declined in the 1850s. Some men tried to farm, but most were unable or unwilling to do so. Young men especially resisted government attempts to make them become farmers, preferring to hunt and trap in the few remaining woodland and prairie areas unoccupied by settlers. And more settlers arrived, some even taking land within the borders of Santee reservations. Tensions increased dramatically, resulting in serious and deadly clashes between Santees and white intruders. In 1854, for instance, two settlers killed a dozen Wahpekutes, most of whom were women or children. Three years later, several Wahpekutes killed 40 whites living in a small settlement. In contrast to the murder of the Wahpekutes, the deaths of the settlers caused an uproar among local politicians and residents. Settlers formed militias and attacked a number of Santee camps. Army troops were sent to capture the Santee men responsible for the killings, but since they were unsuccessful, the settlers' desire for revenge remained unsatisfied.

Pressure continued for more Santee land. Minnesota politicians argued that Santees did not need all their territory because most of them refused to farm it. Ironically, those Indians who did turn their land into farms actually made it more attractive to American settlers. In the words of Kintzing Pritchette, a government agent writing to his superiors in Washington, "[T]he desire of whites for grasping Santee lands increased in proportion as they may have made them valuable by improvement."

In order to negotiate a new treaty and obtain additional Santee territory, Commissioner Mix invited 24 native leaders to Washington, D.C., in 1858. Mix met the delegates, including Wabasha, Shakopee, Wakute, Little Crow, and Mankato. He began by declaring ominously, "I do not wish to frighten or unnecessarily alarm you, but you and your people are now living on the land you occupy by the courtesy of your Great Father." When Mix told the chiefs that the government wanted to acquire half of their reservation located northeast of the Minnesota River, the Santees objected. Little Crow commented, "I recollect that you promised us [in 1854] that we should have this same land forever; and yet now you want to take half of it away. You gave us a paper and we had it explained and now it seems that the Sioux Indians own nothing! We had, we supposed, made a complete treaty," Little Crow continued, "and we were promised a great many things, horses, cattle, flour, plows, and farming utensils, but now it appears that the wind blows it all off."

Mix responded that the federal government would not forever prevent the state of Minnesota from taking Santee land by force, land that, he said, "your Great Father proposes to buy and pay for." Mix's threat produced the desired result. The native delegates signed the treaty ceding all but a 10-mile strip of land on the southwest shore of the Minnesota River and an additional tract nearby. When the U.S. Congress ratified the treaty, it awarded the Santee $266,880, a sum that amounted to 30 cents per acre, even though federal agents in Minnesota thought the land was worth at least five dollars per acre. The Indians actually received only a small portion of the awarded money because nearly all of it was given direct-

"You gave us a paper and we had it explained and now it seems that the Sioux Indians own nothing!" was how Little Crow summed up the situation of his people to the U.S. government in 1858.

ly to American traders for "just debts" supposedly owed by the Santee people.

In addition to the sale of territory, the Treaty of 1858 divided Santee reservations into separate parcels, each consisting of 80 acres. *Allotments* were assigned to individuals or families who agreed to farm, but most native people

On the reservation some Santee Sioux tried to adopt white ways of living, but those who succeeded at farming, for example, found that they had only increased whites' desire for their land.

objected to the division of land because they preferred to own their land in common.

Loss of territory and pressures to farm created tensions in Santee communities. The people were no longer united in purpose or attitude. Some believed that it was best to accommodate the government's demands that they become farmers and adopt an American lifestyle. Consequently, they wore American clothing, lived in single-family houses, and sent their children to mission schools. Other Santees preferred to maintain traditional economies and living arrange- ments as much as possible. These people kept their own clothing and hairstyles, lived in extended-family residences, and followed native religious practices. They deeply resented the Americans' intrusion into their lives and vowed to resist set- tlers' encroachment on their territory. As Big Eagle, a Mdewakanton chief, observed, "The whites are always trying to make the Indians give up their life and live like white men, and the Indians do not want to. If the Indians tried to make the whites live like them, the whites would resist, and it is the same way with many Indians."

THE DISPOSSESSED 65

Government policies worsened the cultural divisions among the Santee. Favors and benefits were granted to farmers and their families but denied to hunters. Even annuities guaranteed by treaty were withheld from men who continued to hunt. Tensions on reservations increased in the early 1860s, caused both by deepening divisions among the Santee and by deteriorating economic conditions. Hunters could not provide enough food for their families; farmers fared just as badly because of extremely cold weather and because a large influx of settlers took the best farmland. By the spring of 1862, many Santees were starving. Local government agents helped farmers by distributing food kept in warehouses at agency headquarters, but hunters were denied provisions.

All Santees looked forward to the scheduled annuity payments so that they could purchase food and goods. But when the money was distributed, American traders stepped forward and demanded that the Indians settle their debts. Although the people had no way of knowing whether the traders' claims were legitimate, most were forced to turn over their entire annuity shares to the merchants.

By summer, the Santees were desperate. Some young men broke into government warehouses to get food for their starving families. Then, on August 17, 1862, several Mdewakanton hunters clashed with a settler family at Acton, Minnesota, killing five people. After the men returned to the reservation and reported what had happened, councils were called to discuss the matter. Long-standing cultural divisions affected the deliberations. Those people who had taken up farming and accepted government policies were largely in favor of offering restitution and surrendering the men responsible for the killings. Young hunters and warriors, however, thought it was time to resist settlers' encroachment on their land and officials' demands that they abandon traditional customs. The young men looked to influential leaders for support, but initially they were rebuffed. Little Crow told them that they could not defeat the Americans, declaring, "We are only little herds of buffaloes left scattered; the great herds that once covered the prairies are no more. The white men are like the locusts when they fly so thick that the whole sky is a snow-storm. You will die like the rabbits when the hungry wolves hunt them."

In the end, though, Little Crow decided to lead the men in what later became known as the Sioux Uprising of 1862. The warriors planned to first rid their reservations of traders, officials, and missionaries. They attacked a government agency center at Redwood, destroying stores and killing about 20 Americans who lived there. Most of the residents, however, were spared, some by the warriors themselves and others by the Santees who opposed the war. When word of the conflict reached nearby Fort Ridgely, Captain John Marsh led a contingent to Redwood. Santee warriors defeated Marsh's troops and then turned to neighboring American settlements along the Minnesota River valley and beyond, as far south as the Iowa border and east to the Mississippi River. In clashes with settlers, the Indians killed more than 400 Americans and took some 100 captives while suffering fewer casualties themselves.

Following the warriors' initial success, other Santees joined their ranks, swelling the number to more than 800. Several chiefs, including Shakopee, Big Eagle, and Gray Bird, threw their support to the war. Although Little Crow hoped for a negotiated settlement with the Americans, he thought the Santees' position would be strengthened if they could defeat the soldiers at Fort Ridgely. The Indians attacked the fort on August 22, inflicting much damage and many casualties but failing to attain their objective.

When the men returned home, dissension arose concerning the future course of action. Some decided to quit fighting, while those who favored the war planned to retreat northward away from concentrations of soldiers and settlers. Little Crow still hoped to reach a negotiated settlement, but by then a force of 1,200 American soldiers, commanded by Colonel Henry Sibley, had arrived at Fort Ridgely. The Santee divided into several groups, some proceeding into the dense woodlands, others making their way north along the Minnesota River. Colonel Sibley sent word to Little Crow that if the Indians released the American captives, he and the Santee leader could talk about settling the conflict without further bloodshed. Although Sibley later admitted that he had no intention of ending the war peacefully, Little Crow offered to release prisoners and negotiate. Sibley never responded, knowing that opposition to the war was growing among the native people.

Toward the end of September, several clashes between Santees and American soldiers occurred, resulting in casualties on both sides. During this period, Indians who opposed the war got control of many of the American captives and later freed them. When it became clear that the Santee could not defeat the American army, Little Crow released the remaining captives and led some 500 warriors and their families westward, seeking safety on the plains. Pursued by Colonel Sibley's soldiers and facing bitterly cold weather and a lack of food, many Santees decided to return to Minnesota. Sibley was unable to reach Little Crow and the contingent that remained with him, but the colonel's troops captured many Santees as they journeyed homeward. In the end, hundreds of Santees were taken prisoner and many others surrendered.

Acting without official approval, Sibley began a series of trials of nearly 400 imprisoned men. When prisoners were brought before military tribunals, many admitted being present at a battle. Their statements were taken as confessions of murder. By the end of the proceedings, 303 men were condemned to death by hanging and were taken to the town of Mankato, Minnesota, to await

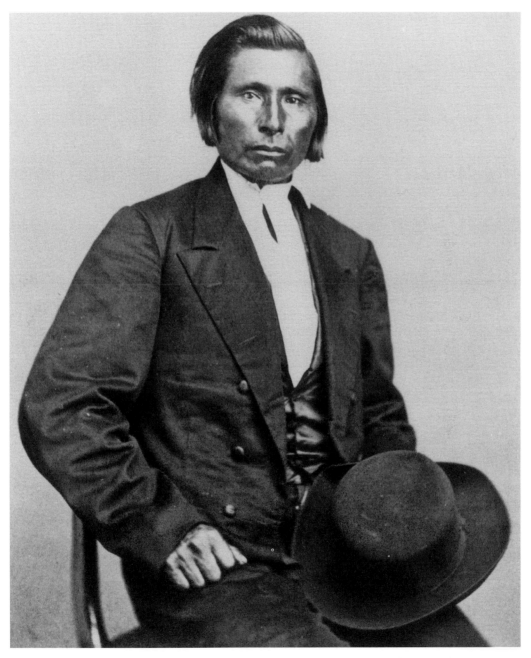

John Otherday, a Santee who was photographed in 1862. Among the nontraditional ways that the U.S. government insisted the Santee adopt in exchange for reservation rights was individual rather than communal land ownership.

Settlers rest while fleeing the violence of the Sioux Uprising of 1862. At the end of the 1840s, there were approximately 6,000 Indians and 6,000 whites in Minnesota. Ten years later, the Indian population was about the same, but the number of whites had risen to more than 150,000.

execution. Questions were raised, however, about the legality of the trials and the quality of evidence used to convict the men. Transcripts of the proceedings were sent to Washington, D.C., for review. President Abraham Lincoln decided to spare most of the men but signed death warrants for 38. They were executed together on December 26, 1862. It was the largest mass execution in American history.

The remaining prisoners were sent to a jail in Davenport, Iowa, where they stayed for three years. During their imprisonment, one-third of the men died from starvation and illness. Many of their wives and children who lived at a nearby camp suffered similar fates. Others were killed by American settlers who raided the defenseless Indians.

While the trials and executions were taking place, Little Crow and his followers sought refuge and support from other native peoples on the plains of the northern United States and southern Canada. Failing this, the Santee group separated. Some stayed on the American plains, others went to Canada, and a few headed east toward Minnesota. In June of 1863, Little Crow and his 16-year-old son, Wowinape, returned to Minnesota. An American farmer who saw them picking raspberries in the woods shot at them, killing Little Crow and wounding his son. At the time, the farmer did not know who the men were; he shot them only because they were Indians. But when Minnesota officials realized the dead man's identity, they gave the farmer a reward of $500. Little Crow's body was mutilated by settlers, and his dismembered bones were put on display at the Minnesota Historical Society in St. Paul.

Although the war had ended and thousands of native people were imprisoned or detained in military camps, Minnesota politicians and residents clamored for the government to expel all Santees from the state. In 1863, the U.S. Senate passed a bill to remove the Santee from Minnesota, thus breaking the terms of treaties previously signed and ratified. Mdewakantons and Wahpekutes, the so-called Lower Sioux, were taken by steamship or

Following the defeat of the Sioux Uprising, some Santees, like this group photographed in Winnipeg, Manitoba, in late 1862, fled to Canada.

These refugees from the Sioux Uprising, photographed at Fort Snelling in 1863, were said to be Little Crow's wife and children.

This Santee Sioux "village" was established by the members of the defeated tribe in captivity in Fort Snelling following the uprising. The photograph was taken on November 13, 1862.

forced to walk to a reservation at Crow Creek in South Dakota. Men who had been imprisoned at Davenport, Iowa, were also sent to Crow Creek. Hundreds of people died during the journey, most from disease or starvation. When the survivors arrived at Crow Creek, they found barren land and few resources. Since the men were barred from leaving the reservation to hunt on the prairies, many people starved to death during the first year. Conditions failed to improve during the

next two years, resulting in further declines in population. After protests by the Santee as well as by missionaries and local agents, federal officials ordered that the natives be moved from Crow Creek to a new site along the Missouri River at Niobrara, Nebraska. Niobrara was hardly an improvement over Crow Creek, however. The Santees' situation was summed up in a report by Hampton Denman, a government agent in Nebraska. "All treaties with these Indians," Denman

On December 26, 1862, a total of 38 Santee Sioux "rebels" were hanged simultaneously from a huge scaffold erected in the town square of Mankato, Minnesota. It was the largest mass execution in U.S. history.

said, "have been abrogated, their annuities forfeited, their splendid reservation of valuable land in Minnesota confiscated by the government, their numbers sadly reduced by starvation and disease; they have been humiliated to the dust."

In 1868, Santee leaders attended a treaty council at Fort Laramie to establish permanent boundaries for their reservation. A rectangular block of land, measuring 12 miles from east to west and 15 miles from north to south, was set as the Santee Reservation. The territory, consisting of 115,075 acres, contained very little good farmland. Although some land was useful for grazing animals, much of it had no economic potential whatsoever. One local government agent described it as "the roughest and least valuable tract of country I have seen in Nebraska."

The fate of the Sisseton and Wahpeton, or Upper Sioux, was similar to that of the Mdewakanton and Wahpekute. Few Sissetons or Wahpetons had taken part in the Sioux War of 1862, but all had reason to fear imprisonment or death at the hands of the American army or Minnesota citizens. They therefore fled onto the plains of the northern United States and Canada, seeking refuge and peace. For several years, they lived on the plains, hunting the few remaining buffalo and gathering wild foods as best they could. Then, in 1867, a delegation of leaders representing Sissetons and Wahpetons in the United States traveled to Washington, D.C., to negotiate for a permanent reservation. They obtained two tracts of land, called the Sisseton and the Devil's Lake reservations, located in Dakota Territory (present-day North and South Dakota). Like the territory of the Santee Reservation in Nebraska, land in the Dakotas was barren and largely unproductive. Living conditions were difficult, resulting in illness and scores of deaths. The population at Sisseton Reservation, for example, numbered 1,637 in 1868 but had declined to 1,498 just two years later.

Leaders of the nearly 2,000 Santees who remained in Canada sought land to establish stable, safe communities for their people. Safety was a critical issue because the American army repeatedly appealed to the Canadian and British governments for permission to enter Canada—then a colony of Great Britain—to attack Santees seeking refuge there. Although permission was refused, the Americans made forays into Canada nonetheless. In one incident in 1864, they kidnapped two chiefs, drugged them with opium and chloroform, and took them to Fort Snelling, where they were executed on November 11, 1865.

In meetings with Canadian officials in Manitoba, Santee leaders recalled the long history of alliance between the Santee and British nations and the service that Santee warriors had given the British cause in the War of 1812. At first, authorities were reluctant to respond to the Indians' requests. But through persistent efforts, Santees eventually obtained land and set up reserves in the provinces of Manitoba and Saskatchewan.

By 1870, just 20 years after signing treaties that guaranteed them land "forever," the Santee were a divided and dispossessed nation. Gone were their former prosperity, vast territory, community cohesion, and political independence. Still, the people were determined to survive in a situation created by forces largely beyond their control. ▲

Santee Sioux gather on their reservation at Niobrara, Nebraska, which one observer described as the "roughest and least valuable tract of country" in the state.

HARD
TIMES

By the 1870s, Santees living in the United States were subjected to pressure from federal and local authorities to alter or abandon their social, economic, and political traditions and replace them with foreign practices and values. Although government policies were supposedly aimed at improving the Santees' lives, in fact the people endured numerous hardships as a result of official actions. Those Santees who rejected American culture and tenaciously followed their own traditions were denied rations and annuities guaranteed by treaties. But even Santees who accepted government programs faced monumental obstacles.

As soon as Santee reservations were established, federal officials urged the people to accept allotments of from 40 to 80 acres for individual or family farms. The allotment program was voluntary but included inducements in the form of benefits and aid. Local authorities encouraged natives to grow wheat, oats, and corn in the hope that surplus crops could be sold to nearby American communities at a profit. However, farming was difficult if not impossible. The land was barren and people lacked necessary equipment. Government agents were often late in delivering plows, livestock, and seed promised in treaties. In addition, extremely cold weather alternated with drought during much of the 1870s and 1880s, ruining crops that had been planted. And infestations of grasshoppers devoured several potential harvests. As a result of crop losses, people suffered from malnutrition and disease. The native population further declined from starvation and epidemics of smallpox and measles.

Lacking resources, the Santee were forced to rely on government rations to survive. But since the distribution of food was often delayed or mismanaged, people continued to suffer.

In order to hasten the Santees' adoption of American culture, the government tried to weaken the influence of hereditary chiefs, many of whom favored maintaining traditional practices. Government agents encouraged the people to ignore the chiefs' advice and institute a system of leadership based on an elected council. Wabasha, the most respected traditional chief at the Santee Reservation, strongly opposed abandoning the native system. Soon after his death in 1876, opposition to the new council subsided. In 1878, a council was elected and charged with managing local affairs—although it had little, if any, real power.

By the 1880s, most Santees had adopted external features of American culture. They wore American clothing and hairstyles, lived in single-family frame houses, attended church services, and sent their children to school. Boarding schools, in fact, became central to the changes taking place. Government authorities hoped that when native children were separated from their parents, they would abandon traditional customs and adopt practices consistent with American ideals. Schools were therefore quickly established on Santee reservations. The most successful and long-lived institution was the Santee Normal Training School, located on the reservation in Nebraska. It attracted students from all Santee communities as well as from

Yankton and Teton reservations in the Dakotas.

Santee schools were funded by the federal government and operated by Christian missionaries under agreements assigning reservations to ministers from various denominations. Schools on the Santee Reservation were run by members of the Congregational church, those on the Sisseton Reservation were managed by Presbyterians, and schools at Devil's Lake were operated by Catholics. Even after the government stopped funding mission schools, education on Santee reservations remained largely under the control of ministers and priests.

When schools were opened, instruction was given in the native Dakota language even though federal Indian policy mandated that all native children be taught only in English. An order issued by Commissioner John Atkins in 1887 stated, "The instruction of the Indians in the vernacular [their native language] is not only of no use to them, but is detrimental to the cause of their education and civilization, and no school will be permitted on the reservation in which the English language is not exclusively taught." Threatened with an end to federal financing, administrators of Santee schools obeyed Atkins's order.

In addition to banning the use of native languages, authorities wanted schools to change children's attitudes. A federal supervisor at the Santee Reservation warned teachers that "no school children should be permitted to be spectators at [traditional ceremonial]

Graduates of the Santee Normal School on the Santee Reservation at Niobrara, in present-day Knox County, Nebraska.

dances as the Office thinks it would be better to keep their ideas away from these old-time customs."

After years of missionary activity in schools and churches, most Santees were at least nominally Christian by the end of the 19th century. They attended regular church services, sang hymns translated into Dakota, and heard sermons delivered in their native language by both Santee and American ministers. Still, some aspects of native religious belief and practice persisted. Most Santees continued to believe in the Great Mystery of powerful spirit forces that pervaded the natural world. And they participated in ceremonial dances, feasts, and *giveaways*.

Economic problems remained serious in the last years of the century. Indeed, many problems were compounded by government policies. In 1887, the U.S. Congress passed the General Allotment Act, which ordered

This photograph of Santee schoolchildren at the Lower Sioux Agency in Morton, Minnesota, in 1901 illustrates the ways in which reservation schooling operated as an agent of forced acculturation. The students are all wearing non-Indian clothing and have their hair cut in a non-Indian fashion. No pictures of great Indian leaders adorn the classroom; instead, photos of President William McKinley, Vice President Theodore Roosevelt, Abraham Lincoln, and Governor Gus Van Sant watch over the pupils.

the division of all federal reservations into allotments, a practice that until then had been voluntary. Afterward, Santees were forced to accept individual parcels of land, usually consisting of 80 or 160 acres. The process of allotment split up communally owned land and decreased the economic potential of farming. In addition, the Allotment Act provided that whatever land remained after parcels were assigned should be declared surplus and made available to American homesteaders. As elsewhere throughout the United States, Santee reservations lost hundreds of thousands of acres to outsiders. After allotment, people at the Santee Reservation retained 71,784 acres of land but lost 42,160 acres to homesteaders. More than half of the original Sisseton Reservation was sold after allotment. There, Indians were allotted 310,711 acres while 573,872 acres went to outsiders. As their land holdings declined dramatically, many Santees gave up all efforts to grow crops and instead leased their land to American farmers, who had more capital to buy and maintain machinery and livestock.

During the late 19th century, Santee economies benefited for a time from new sources of money. Federal courts ruled favorably on several land-claims cases and awarded small cash payments to Indians for land illegally taken earlier in the century. And Santees earned income from wage work and services rendered to nearby communities. They supplied military posts with timber and sold buffalo bones from carcasses littering the prairies to manufacturers of bone china dishware. Nevertheless, the words of a federal agent at Devil's Lake applied equally to all Santee reservations: "The Indians are surrounded by disadvantages, and their nearest neighbors are poverty, hunger, and failure."

Not all Santees resided on federal reservations in the late 19th century, however. In 1869, a group of 25 families left the Santee Reservation in Nebraska and founded a small colony at Flandreau, South Dakota, along the Big Sioux River. Hoping to become independent farmers, they faced the same economic and environmental difficulties as did their relatives on reservations. In addition, Flandreau residents had to renounce their tribal affiliation in order to receive legal title to land. Since their land was not protected by treaties or statutes, it was subject to taxation. Some people sold their acreage because they could not pay the excessive taxes that were levied against them. While the population at Flandreau declined, those who stayed gradually improved their economic situation. Residents worked at a nearby pipestone quarry and made stone pipes, rings, and other small objects for sale to neighboring American communities.

A second group of nonreservation Santees consisted of nearly 400 people who remained in their homeland in southern Minnesota. This group included a small number who had never relocated from ancestral lands to the northern Minnesota reservations established in 1853. A larger segment of the population had gone to the reservations in the 1850s but did not leave when the majority of Santees were forcibly removed to Nebraska after the Sioux Uprising of 1862. These people either had not taken part in the war or had actively opposed it. By congressional legislation passed in 1863, the Santee were permitted to stay in Minnesota and received 80 acres of land per family or single individual. Two years later, Congress granted the Indians $7,500 to help set up farms.

The number of Santees in Minnesota increased as a result of immigration from reservations in Nebraska and the Dakotas. The people lived in small settlements scattered in the southern portion of the state. Their locations shifted several times as surrounding American towns grew and engulfed them. By the end of the 19th century, the Minnesota Santee were concentrated at Birch Coulee, Prairie Island, and Prior Lake. Although the Indians had to sell some of their territory, additional acreage was purchased with funds provided by land-claims settlements. The people's financial situation improved slightly when native women began manufacturing lace for sale to nearby American communities. Still, farming was the mainstay of their economy, subject as always to drought, cold, and infestations of insects.

In addition to those living in the United States, nearly 2,000 Santees resided on reserves in the Canadian provinces of Manitoba and Saskatchewan. These people had sought refuge in Canada during or after the Sioux Uprising of 1862. At first, they lived in small, dispersed settlements and followed traditional pursuits. From 1875 to 1893, leaders of several Santee communities negotiated with Canadian officials to obtain land for permanent reserves. In contrast to the pattern imposed on Santees in the United States, the Canadian Santee were able to maintain separate settlements based on traditional band divisions under the leadership of hereditary chiefs. Santees selected land at sites near the Assiniboine, Qu'Appelle, and Saskatchewan rivers. In all, eight reserves were established: Oak River, Oak Lake, Birdtail Creek, Turtle Mountain, Standing Buffalo, Whitecap, Sturgeon Lake, and Wahpeton. The Santee received land according to a formula providing 80 acres to each family of five. Officials gave assurances that Santees could acquire additional land should their needs increase, but these promises were rarely fulfilled.

Once reserves were established, the people gradually adopted farming as the basis of their economy. They built up stocks of cattle, pigs, chickens, and sheep. When harvests were good, the Santee prospered. A Canadian official, G. P. Wadsworth, visited the reserve at Birdtail Creek and commented, "Upon reaching my destination, I could not help making comparisons between the Indians' crops on the Reserve, and those of settlers; the verdict was strongly in favour of the Indians."

However, Santee farmers faced severe environmental problems, principally drought, cold weather, and grasshopper plagues. Approximately half of the residents left their reserves, at least temporarily, to hunt, fish, and gather wild foods. Those people who remained survived the difficult years of the late 19th century by combining several subsistence strategies. In addition to farming, they sold timber and hand-

Young Santee women are taught to sew at the Indian School on the reservation in Flandreau, South Dakota, early in the 20th century.

crafts at army posts and Canadian settlements. And they worked in a variety of jobs to earn cash incomes. In fact, Santee labor was in great demand and was relatively well paid. Men worked as farm laborers, construction workers, and lumbermen. Women were employed as domestic workers in the homes of Canadian settlers and officials.

Some Canadian Santee bands lived too far north to permit farming beyond simple household gardens. They therefore had to depend on other subsistence resources. In addition to hunting, fishing, and gathering, the people of the Whitecap Reserve in Saskatchewan built up cattle stocks for commercial sale. For a time the market for cattle,

Sioux members of the baseball team in Flandreau.

spurred by the export of beef to Great Britain, was strong. But because demand and prices fluctuated dramatically, cattle raising did not provide a stable income.

Santees living in Canada adopted many features of Canadian culture. They lived in frame houses, wore Canadian clothing, opened schools, and attended Christian services. At the same time, they continued such traditional activities as feasts, dances, and giveaways. Although local officials and

missionaries disapproved of these practices, the government did not directly interfere with Santee cultural life until the 1890s. Then, Hayter Reed, commissioner of the Department of Indian Affairs, imposed rigid guidelines on native communities in order to force people to abandon ancestral customs. Native religious and secular ceremonies were outlawed, and participants were punished with fines and prison sentences. In addition, officials pressured Santees to break up extended-family households and ignore traditional communal responsibilities. Since local agents observed that Santee families often pooled their resources to buy modern farm equipment and depended on networks of relatives to help plant and harvest crops, Commissioner Reed denied Santees the right to purchase modern machinery and insisted that they use outmoded and inefficient equipment. For example, Reed demanded that Santee farmers cut grain with scythes rather than with mechanical mowers and reapers and that they use hand rakes and forks instead of modern threshers.

Under Reed's orders, Santees had to obtain official permits to work or travel outside their reserves or to sell produce, firewood, or cattle. The permit system had social and religious consequences as well because local agents routinely denied work or commercial licenses to anyone known or even suspected of participating in traditional ceremonial activities. When Santees protested the rules, their objections were immediately dismissed. Indeed, three chiefs who were en route by train to the Canadian capital of Ottawa to lodge complaints were forcibly removed from the train and returned to their reserve.

Federal regulations undermined the Santee's economy by stifling their ability to make decisions, improve their technology and crop yield, and compete freely in the labor and product markets springing up around them. A sympathetic Manitoba newspaper criticized government policy in an article printed in 1894: "They farm their own land, work hard all summer, and through the obnoxious orders are not allowed the full benefit of the fruit of their own labour. They are thus placed at a disadvantage in competition with their white neighbors."

As the 19th century ended, the Santee's economic growth was blocked by federal and local policies. The people's economy and living conditions deteriorated, in stark contrast to the growing prosperity of Canadian farms in their vicinity.

At the start of the 20th century, conditions for American and Canadian Santees were similar. People lived in rural areas, dependent on farming in terrain that was largely unproductive without investments of capital and machinery. In the United States, the Santees' poverty increased as more land was lost through sales to American farmers. These sales were made possible by terms of the 1887 General Allotment Act, which permitted individual owners to sell land to outsiders after a period of 25 years. American farmers bought up adjacent allotments and made profits from large, consolidated holdings that they purchased. In contrast, native farmers did not have the capital to buy land, machinery, or livestock and therefore could not farm productively. In addition, as years passed, most of the original allotments came under joint ownership through patterns of inheritance that gave all heirs equal shares in a deceased's land. Since few Santee heirs could afford to buy out the other partners, and since dividing the land would not have given anyone enough acreage to support themselves, people often decided to sell their allotment and divide the proceeds. "Our white neighbors are always ready to give us advice and claim that they are doing so for our personal benefit," a resident of the Santee Reservation wrote to a Nebraska newspaper in 1911. "They tell us that we are thoroughly competent to handle our own affairs and endorse us for the titles to our allotments, but when our land is sold and the money spent, Where-Do-We-Stand?"

While Santees were losing what little land they owned, the federal government was reducing or ending appropriations for their benefit—appropriations that had been guaranteed by treaties. Increasing poverty led to higher rates of malnutrition and disease. The population of Santee reservations declined, due both to higher death rates and to migration away from the communities. Although the people received several payments from successful land-claims suits in the early 1900s, the amounts were too small to make significant long-term improvements in their lives. Indeed, in 1926, Edgar Howard, a Nebraska member of the U.S. House of Representatives, visited the Santee Reservation and described conditions there as "deplorable beyond words."

Living conditions for the Santee did not begin to improve until the 1930s. At that time, John Collier, commissioner of Indian Affairs, instituted new policies designed to aid native communities. Collier was responding to a survey report issued in 1928 that documented high levels of poverty, unemployment, and poor health on reservations throughout the United States. The survey, called the Meriam Report after its principal investigator, recommended increased funding to help Indian economies become self-sufficient; to construct new housing, roads, and sewage systems; and to improve educational and medical services. Collier began implementing the report's recommendations by urging Congress to pass the Indian Reorganization Act in 1934, which provided funds for purchases of land and improvements on reservations.

Santees used the money to buy back some land that had been lost through sales to outsiders. The Santee Reservation in Nebraska added 3,368 acres to the scant 3,132 that remained after decades of losses amounting to more than 68,000 acres. The people at Sisseton and Devil's Lake also made purchases with funds provided by Congress. Santees living in Flandreau, South Dakota, bought 2,100 acres and, at the same time, successfully petitioned the government to change their legal status from an Indian colony to a federal reservation. With reservation status, native land was protected from future sale or taxation. Although Santees living in Minnesota did not form reservations, they were officially recognized as Indian communities and were permitted to purchase additional land. Twelve

At Morton, Minnesota, some Santee women became skilled lace makers. They were trained in the craft by Sybil Morton, an Episcopal missionary who also taught lace making to Ojibwa women.

Santee men learn the rudiments of engine repair at the Flandreau Indian School in the 1920s.

hundred acres were added to the holdings at Birch Coulee, while the Prairie Island community increased by 400 acres and the Granite Falls community by 700 acres.

In addition to provisions regarding land purchases, the Indian Reorganization Act enabled reservation communities to establish tribal councils with rights of self-government. Although the people won some power to make decisions and control planning and finances, final authority actually rested with the Bureau of Indian Affairs in Washington, D.C. Still, Santees voted to set up governing councils and gradually assumed more responsibility for local management.

Finally, under John Collier's administration, federal Indian policy reversed former bans on the use of native languages in schools and ended pressures against the performance of native dances and ceremonies. The people were encouraged to maintain their traditional languages and customs as they saw fit.

Although Santee reservations added land in the 1930s, the people's economic situation improved only slightly. They still lacked enough acreage to grow the surpluses of crops needed to obtain cash incomes. Funds for more land purchases dried up in the 1940s with the outbreak of World War II. And opportunities for wage work were minimal because reservations were situated in rural areas far from centers of industry and employment. In contrast, Santees in Minnesota found jobs in towns and cities near their homes. As a result, their communities were more prosperous than those in Nebraska and the Dakotas. However, compared with their non-Indian neighbors, the Minnesota Santees suffered poor living conditions, the legacy of decades of mistreatment and discrimination.

During the first half of the 20th century, many changes occurred in the lives of Canadian Santees. Most residents of reserves attempted to make their livings from farming but had to cope with numerous problems. Shortage of land was a major difficulty. Santees could not buy additional acreage because the surrounding countryside was occupied by Canadian farmers. As Canadian populations grew, competition for land increased, raising purchase prices well beyond the Santees' reach. In addition, several Santee reserves were completely eliminated after years of pressure by government authorities who wanted to consolidate native communities and at the same time make land available for the growing Canadian population. In 1908, for instance, the Turtle Mountain Reserve was officially ended by government decree, and its residents were moved to the Oak Lake Reserve. Members of the Turtle Mountain band were told that they would receive individual payments as well as interest on money obtained from the sale of their reserve. But when the land was sold at auction for a sum of only $6,329, David Laird, commissioner of the Department of Indian Affairs, concluded that "the sale of the reserve having yielded so much less than was expected at the time of the surrender it is not worthwhile placing anything to their credit, on which they could draw interest." And after the department deducted expenses incurred in relocating Turtle Mountain residents to Oak Lake, no money remained for individual payments to the Santees.

In 1928, the Santee reserve near the city of Portage la Prairie, Manitoba, was abandoned after the government convinced residents to relocate to a new community called Long Plain. Official policy favored giving Santee territory to the growing city of Portage la Prairie. Once the Santees relocated to the remote Long Plain Reserve, they had to

Sioux women await the apportionment of rations on the reservation. Despite the professed dedication of missionaries, educators, and government officials to the "improvement" of the Indians, life on the reservation invariably meant a decline in self-sufficiency.

begin all over again with the difficult task of turning their land into farms.

At the reserves of Oak River and Oak Lake in southern Manitoba, Santee farmers prospered when markets for their products were strong. However, the worldwide economic depression of the 1930s severely undermined their security. And as farm machinery became more expensive, only people

with large tracts of land could afford to invest the capital needed to purchase and maintain equipment.

Shortages of land and money gradually resulted in the economic stratification of Santees living on the reserves. Land on Indian reserves could not be sold to outsiders, but people could sell rights to use their land to other members of the band. Those with financial assets bought up use rights from their less fortunate neighbors and then purchased modern farm equipment, increased their crop yields, and earned good incomes. In contrast, people with few means held on to small parcels of land and were barely able to provide enough food for their families. Others abandoned farming altogether and took jobs as farm laborers both on and off their reserve. Men also worked in lumber mills, railroad yards, and manufacturing plants, while women found employment as factory workers or domestics in Canadian homes.

On some Santee reserves, people tried to earn incomes by raising cattle for commercial sale. At the reserves of Standing Buffalo and White Cap, cattle sales were strong in the early years of the 20th century. But on both reserves, people lost access to grazing land over the course of a few decades. By 1907, Santees at the Standing Buffalo Reserve were denied permission to graze herds on nearby government ranges because the land was turned over to Canadian ranchers. Once Santees were limited to

grazing animals on their small reserve, they had to sell off the majority of their herds and soon abandoned what had appeared to be a stable economic strategy. And at White Cap, land that residents had acquired with temporary permits was lost in the 1930s, thus destroying their ability to raise large numbers of animals. They too were forced to give up a once-profitable enterprise.

While the economies of Santee communities in the United States and Canada were vastly changed from earlier centuries and most of their social and religious practices were abandoned, some traditional customs and beliefs remained. Extended-family relationships were the backbone of support for people in times of need. Relatives pooled their resources and depended on one another's labor. Feasting, accompanied by generous giveaways of food, clothing, and ornaments, was an important means of recognizing community bonds. And both ceremonial and social dances continued as expressions of traditional culture and the Santee's desire to retain their unique identity. ▲

A dancer at the annual powwow held by the Shakopee Mdewakanton Dakota Community at its reservation near Prior Lake Community. More than 10,000 people usually attend this event.

7

THE
SANTEE
TODAY

In both the United States and Canada, the second half of the 20th century began for Santees with the steady erosion of their land base and decreases in the numbers of people living on the reservations. But it is ending with the expansion of economic resources, improvements in living conditions, and the promise of continued growth.

During the 1940s and 1950s, many Santees left their reservations in Nebraska and the Dakotas because they did not have enough land to earn adequate incomes from farming. The deteriorating economic situation, substandard housing, and poor educational opportunities also prompted people to move away from rural communities. The most serious population loss occurred at the Santee Reservation, which experienced a decline of 60 percent during the period from 1940 to 1960. By 1962, only 299 people, most of them elderly, remained there. Younger people hoped to find jobs in towns and cities in the Midwest and elsewhere in the United States.

Then, in the late 1960s and 1970s, money for needed improvements on reservations became available. Funds from federal antipoverty programs helped poor communities build new housing, roads, schools, and other public facilities. Housing projects not only gave people better living quarters but also created construction and maintenance jobs. Similar benefits accompanied the building of roads, schools, community centers, and health clinics. Once living conditions improved and jobs were available, some Santees returned to the reservations, resulting in slow but steady increases in population in the last 20 years, although the number of reservation residents remains much lower than the number of enrolled tribal members. Approximately half of the enrolled tribal members now live on the Devil's Lake, Lake Traverse (formerly called Sisseton), and Flandreau reservations in the Dakotas, while an additional one-fifth of enrolled members live on the Santee Reservation in Nebraska. The 1990 census lists the populations of the reservations as follows: Lake Traverse, 2,821; Devil's Lake, 2,676; Santee, 425; and Flandreau, 249.

In addition to jobs created by the construction of roads and facilities, Santees find employment on reservations in offices of tribal governments and local branches of the Bureau of Indian Affairs and the Public Health Service. People work in health clinics, day-care centers, and schools delivering expanded medical, educational, and

The Dakotah Sport and Fitness Center on the Prior Lake Reservation was completed in late 1994. The center boasts two full-size gymnasiums, racquetball and squash courts, indoor tracks, a firing range, a year-round skating rink, a pool, and rock-climbing facilities.

Young traditional dancers at the Mdewakanton Dakota powwow. In 1969, just 13 Santees were living on the Prior Lake tribal lands. Today more than 200 Sioux live on the reservation, which despite being the smallest in Minnesota is one of the most successful financially.

social services. The communities have their own primary and secondary schools whose curricula include Santee history and culture and the Dakota language. They have accredited colleges as well, including the Santee campus of the Nebraska Indian Community College at Santee, the Sisseton-Wahpeton Community College at Lake Traverse, and the Little Hoop Community College at Devil's Lake.

Tribal councils operate a number of businesses that employ community members and earn income for the tribe. The people at the Santee Reservation run a 2,400-acre ranch with more than 600 head of cattle. The Flandreau Reservation has several tribal enterpris-

The pool at the Dakotah Sport and Fitness facility. The reservation's incredible financial success has been due in large part to revenues from legalized gambling on tribal grounds.

es, including a motel, a housing project, and a convenience store. And at Devil's Lake Reservation, the tribe operates stores, laundries, and a credit union. In addition, the tribe owns two factories, the Sioux Manufacturing Company and Dakota Tribal Industries, that manufacture equipment for the U.S. Department of Defense. Dakota Tribal Industries was named "Minority Business of the Year" in 1990.

Private industry has recently been attracted to sites on or near reservations, providing another significant source of jobs. The Becton-Dickenson pharmaceutical company has a manufacturing plant on the Santee Reservation. The Lake Traverse Reservation hosts plants operated by Power Sentry, an electronics company, and Dakota Western, a manufacturer of plastic bags. Lake Traverse residents also work in the town of Watertown, South Dakota, located some 60 miles from the reservation, at a chicken-processing plant and a factory that produces quilts.

Santees living in Minnesota are employed in both the public and private sectors in nearby towns and cities. Their populations have remained fairly stable in the last half century. Census figures for 1990 for the four communities report 225 residents at Lower Sioux (formerly called Birch Coulee), 153 at the Shakopee Mdewakanton Community (formerly Prior Lake), 56 at Prairie Island, and 43 at Upper Sioux (formerly Granite Falls).

Minnesota Santees have recently increased their incomes by opening gambling establishments in their settlements. Residents of the Shakopee Mdewakanton Community were the first to enter this highly profitable business. Their right to operate gaming parlors is protected by a U.S. Supreme Court decision ruling that Indian communities can maintain such facilities without any interference from state or county authorities. In 1982, Shakopee Mdewakantons opened the Little Six Bingo Palace and attracted thousands of players from the major centers of St. Paul and Minneapolis as well as from other cities in the Midwest. In the words of Norman Crooks, then the Shakopee's tribal chairman, it was "darn near a Utopia." Gross income from Little Six grew to $18 million by 1986. Profits are distributed according to a fixed formula that divides the largest share, 54.5 percent, among the residents of Shakopee, who receive individual payments monthly. The second share of profits, amounting to 45 percent, is designated for tribal programs. Within a few years, the tribe used these funds to build a medical and dental facility, a day-care center, a cultural center, and a tribal office complex. The third share, 0.5 percent, pays for expenses associated with the gaming business.

Once it became clear that Little Six was an economic success, other Minnesota Santees opened similar establishments. Profits are divided by various formulas in the different communities, but all include payments to individuals and funds for the tribe. In 1985, Santees added high-stakes casino gambling to the bingo games already in operation. Players came by the thousands from as far away as Chicago, St. Louis, Kansas City, and Winnipeg, Canada. The largest facility is the Mystic Lake Casino, operated by Shakopee Mdewakantons since 1992. According to Leonard Prescott, the tribal chairman, the share of profits distributed to every Shakopee resident in 1993 amounted to about $4,000 each month.

Although native people throughout the United States are divided about the relative advantages and drawbacks of casino gambling on their land, Santees have benefited from the profits earned. In addition to per capita distributions to community members and jobs created for residents, tribal governments have made improvements and expanded services for the people. Other local businesses have benefited as well, since

Santee veterans of service in the U.S. military mingle with the traditional dancers at the Shakopee Mdewakanton Dakota Community powwow.

tourists and players spend money in shops, restaurants, and hotels near the casinos.

In the 1990s, Santee reservations in the Dakotas also opened gaming par- lors, but because of their rural locations they have not been as profitable as those in Minnesota. Still, they provide resi- dents with jobs and funds that have been used for local improvements.

Land under tribal ownership has increased markedly on all Santee reservations, especially since 1984, when Congress passed legislation to regulate inheritance of land on Indian reserva-tions. The heirship bill limits inheritance of land to close relatives and states that shares must consist of at least 2.5 acres. If a deceased owner has no close relatives who are members of the tribe or the inherited shares amount to less than the acreage permitted, the land reverts to tribal ownership. Federal law also gives tribes the right of eminent domain in order "to eliminate fractional heirship interests, to consolidate tribal interests in land, to develop agriculture, and for other public purposes." As a result of legislation, tribal land at the Devil's Lake Reservation, for example, has jumped from 650 acres in 1960 to about 27,000 acres in 1993.

One of the proudest achievements of the residents of the Shakopee Mdewakanton Dakota Reservation is the Playworks child-care facility, which opened its doors in January 1995. Among its unique features, Playworks boasts the largest indoor slide in the country and is open 24 hours a day.

The economic success of the Shakopee Mdewakanton Dakota Reservation offers the promise of a bright future for young residents such as this man. The community is currently able to offer all its members total medical and dental coverage free of charge, as well as a comprehensive tuition-assistance program for those who wish to pursue a college education.

A $4 million investment, Playworks is perhaps the most ambitious child-care facility of its kind in the country. As such, it represents an enormous commitment on the part of the Mdewakanton Sioux to their children's future.

As in the United States, the economies of the Canadian Santees have expanded in the latter half of the 20th century. Few people earn livings from farming because of the scarcity of land and the high cost of modern technology. Instead, increases in Santees' incomes and improvements in their standard of living have resulted from greater participation in wage work. Some Santees have jobs in band offices, health clinics, schools, and small businesses located on their reserves. The majority, many with advanced technical and academic degrees, find employment in a wide range of occupations in nearby towns and cities such as Brandon and Portage la Prairie, Manitoba, and Saskatoon and Prince Albert, Saskatchewan.

Canadian reserves have experienced some declines in population because of the attraction of job markets distant from native communities. Still, approximately three-fifths of enrolled band members reside on reserves. According to the 1992 Canadian census, the populations of the reserves in Manitoba are as follows: Long Plain Sioux, 903; Oak Lake, 373; Birdtail Sioux, 336; and Dakota Tipi, 141. The Wahpeton Reserve in Saskatchewan has a population of 146.

Although recent decades have brought economic and occupational growth for the Santee, members of the Prairie Island Community in Minnesota have also faced a potential environmental and public-safety threat. In the late 1960s, Northern States Power, a regional power company, built a nuclear generating plant adjacent to the native community. At first, the people did not object because they did not realize the health and safety risks that the plant posed. But by the 1980s, concerns arose about potential contamination from radioactive emissions in the event of an accident at the plant and from leakage of stored hazardous waste.

Further controversy arose in the early 1990s when Northern States Power obtained approval from the Environmental Quality Board to situate a storage facility for spent nuclear fuel next to the Prairie Island Community. At the same time, a study by the Minnesota Department of Health confirmed that radioactive gases emitted from the power plant were increasing the Santees' risk of cancer to six times the state standard. The study warned that the risk would increase further if radioactive waste were stored nearby. The native people immediately began legal efforts to block construction of the storage site. In order to educate the Minnesota public about the issue, they initiated a media campaign, including television advertisements that began, "Northern States Power doesn't want you to hear this." All four of the major networks in the Minneapolis–St. Paul area refused to broadcast the ad.

The Santees' fears about contamination were compounded when a low-level incident occurred in 1992. Although federal officials assured the Santees that public safety had not been threatened, William Hardacker, a lawyer for the Indians, commented that the "Prairie Island community will always have serious questions about the operation of this plant." Shortly afterward, workers discovered that a water line from the plant had been damaged, resulting in leakage of radioactive tritium into people's private wells.

The Santees' attempts to stop construction of the proposed storage site proceeded through legal channels. Contradictory rulings were issued by various regulatory commissions and district courts. Finally, the Minnesota Supreme Court ruled in 1993 that the storage facility could not be built unless the Minnesota legislature explicitly granted permission to the power company. Legislative action has not yet taken place.

The activities of the people at Prairie Island demonstrate a growing sense of community among Santees. The people's pride in their present accomplishments is matched by pride in their history and cultural traditions. Santees in Nebraska and the Dakotas host annual celebrations that attract members of all Santee communities who come to participate in public dances, feasts, and giveaways. Santees living in Manitoba and Saskatchewan maintain some traditional customs while also participating in rural and urban Canadian life. Members of extended families cooperate in work on the reserves and pool their resources to help each other in times of need. People continue to hold ceremonial and social festivals accompanied by dances and giveaways. And the Dakota language is spoken by many Canadian Santees.

Finally, in Mankato, Minnesota, the site of the mass execution of Santee prisoners in 1862, an event that began as a small gathering dedicated to the memory of the native men who fought and died for their people has grown into the annual Mah-Kato Powwow, attended by more than 5,000 people each year. In the 1960s, Amos Owen, then tribal chairman of Prairie Island, conducted a yearly ritual of respect for the slain prisoners. Owen's efforts to honor the men led in 1975 to a Day of Reconciliation, sponsored by the native People's Bicentennial Commission and the American Indian Movement, a native-rights organization. At a rite marking the day, Norman Blue, chairman of the Lower Sioux Community, read the names of the 38 men in the Dakota language. The ceremony ended with traditional songs memorializing the executed warriors.

The Day of Reconciliation was later followed by a Year of Reconciliation, declared by Minnesota governor Rudy Perpich in 1986. On December 26, the anniversary of the mass executions, runners participated in a run from Fort Snelling to Mankato, retracing the final journey of the doomed prisoners. During the year, the remains of 31 men and women who had died in the 1860s in prison and nearby camps at Davenport, Iowa, were returned by an Iowa museum for burial in the cemetery of the Lower Sioux Community. The burial was accompanied by traditional ceremonies, prayers, and songs. Six years later, the remains of 34 Santees were obtained from the Smithsonian Institution in Washington, D.C., for burial in native lands.

The Santee have traveled a long, difficult road since the middle of the 19th century, when their ancestral lands were confiscated and their lives changed forever. But with determination and pride, they have survived as a people and have forged a unique identity combining traditional and contemporary cultures. ▲

BIBLIOGRAPHY

Bonvillain, Nancy. *The Teton Sioux.* New York: Chelsea House, 1994.

Force, Roland W., and Maryanne Tefft Force. *The American Indians.* New York: Chelsea House, 1996.

Hoover, Herbert T. *The Yankton Sioux.* New York: Chelsea House, 1988.

Maxwell, James A., ed. *America's Fascinating Indian Heritage.* Pleasantville, NY: Reader's Digest Association, Inc., 1978.

Taylor, Colin F. *The Plains Indians.* London: Salamander Books, 1994.

Waldman, Carl. *Atlas of the North American Indian.* New York: Facts on File Publications, 1985.

THE SANTEE SIOUX AT A GLANCE

TRIBE   *Santee, Isante, or Dakota*

CULTURE AREA   *Great Plains*

GEOGRAPHY   *Historically, the entire state of Minnesota, concentrated in the southern part of the state and around the Mississippi and Minnesota rivers; also ranging west into eastern South Dakota and north into Canada. There are currently four reservations and communities in Minnesota, two in South Dakota, one in North Dakota, and one in Nebraska, along with Canadian reserves in Manitoba and Saskatchewan.*

LINGUISTIC FAMILY   *Siouan (Macro-Siouan phylum, Santee-Yankton dialect)*

CURRENT POPULATION   *Recent estimates place Santee population at approximately 20,000, distributed as follows: 7,000 in native communities and on reservations in Minnesota, Nebraska, and the Dakotas; 3,000 on Canadian reserves in Manitoba and Saskatchewan; 10,000 off-reservation in the United States and Canada.*

FIRST CONTACT   *The party led by French trader-explorers Paul Radisson and Medard Chouart des Groseilliers, 1660*

FEDERAL STATUS   *The Santee are a federally recognized tribe. Although Mdewakantons, Sisseton-Wahpetons, and Wahpekutes are all Santee people, these distinct tribal bands maintain strong individual identities. Many Santee—most notably members of the Shakopee Mdewakanton Community in Minnesota—benefit from the operation of gaming parlors on tribal lands, where gambling is not subject to government interference.*

GLOSSARY

allotment A parcel of land assigned to reservation Indians. The federal government hoped that allotments, which were given to individuals or families, would induce private farming, effectively ending the Sioux tradition of sharing land and resources.

amorphous Having no real or apparent solid form.

annuity A sum of goods, services, and cash to be delivered each year to Native Americans according to the terms of treaties between the United States and individual tribes. Sioux people were promised annuities for an average of 50 years.

clan A group of people who claim common ancestry.

communal Participated in or shared by all members of a group.

giveaway A customary lavishing of gifts by the host family of a Sioux feast or dance.

herald An official announcer or messenger.

hull To shuck the outer covering from a fruit or seed.

oratory The art of eloquent and effective public speaking.

pemmican Dried meat pounded into a powder and mixed with melted fat and berries.

polygamy The practice of being married to more than one spouse at a time.

powwow A traditional outdoor social festival featuring dancing.

sweat lodge Small enclosed hut where Native Americans ritually purified themselves through sweats, usually induced by steam heat.

Takuwakan Sioux word meaning "Great Mystery," which refers to the spirit powers inhabiting people, animals, and some seemingly inanimate, or lifeless, objects.

travois Plowlike vessel used to transport belongings during migration. It consisted of two wooden slats attached to the sides of a dog or horse, with a basket suspended in the middle to hold valuables.

vision quest A solitary journey into the woods or prairies during which a seeker stays awake and fasts for several days, hoping to be visited and instructed by a spirit being. Young Santee men and women went on vision quests as a rite of passage into adulthood.

INDEX

PICTURE CREDITS

NANCY BONVILLAIN has a Ph.D. in anthropology from Columbia University. Dr. Bonvillain has written a grammar book and dictionary of the Mohawk language as well as *The Hopi* (1994), *Black Hawk* (1994), *The Inuit* (1995), and *The Zuni* (1995) for Chelsea House. She has recently finished work on *Women and Men: Cultural Constructs of Gender*.

FRANK W. PORTER III, general editor of INDIANS OF NORTH AMERICA, is director of the Chelsea House Foundation for American Indian Studies. He holds a B.A., M.A., and Ph.D. from the University of Maryland. He has done extensive research concerning the Indians of Maryland and Delaware and is the author of numerous articles on their history, archaeology, geography, and ethnography. He was formerly director of the Maryland Commission on Indian Affairs and American Indian Research and Resource Institute, Gettysburg, Pennsylvania, and he has received grants from the Delaware Humanities Forum, the Maryland Committee for the Humanities, the Ford Foundation, and the National Endowment for the Humanities, among others. Dr. Porter is the author of *The Bureau of Indian Affairs* in the Chelsea House KNOW YOUR GOVERNMENT series.

Library Media Center
Willowcreek Middle School

FLYING GUNSHIP:
The AC-130 Spectre

Kevin J. Fitzpatrick

Children's Press
High Interest Books
A Division of Grolier Publishing
New York / London / Hong Kong / Sydney
Danbury, Connecticut

Book Design: Nelson Sa
Contributing Editor: Mark Beyer
Photo Credits: Cover © Aero Graphics, Inc./Corbis; pp. 5, 6, 10 © George Hall/Corbis; p. 12 © Leif Skoogfors/Corbis; pp. 15, 19, 21 © George Hall/Corbis; pp. 23, 24 © Photri-Microstock; p. 26 © AFP/Corbis; pp. 29, 31, 32 © Photri-Microstock; p. 34 © George Hall/Corbis; p. 36 © Photri-Microstock; p. 38 © George Hall/Corbis; pp. 40, 41 © Photri-Microstock.

Visit Children's Press on the Internet at:
http://publishing.grolier.com

Library of Congress Cataloging-in-Publication Data

Fitzpatrick, Kevin J.
    Flying gunship : the AC-130 Spectre / by Kevin J. Fitzpatrick.
        p. cm. – (High-tech military weapons)
    Includes bibliographical references and index.
    Summary: Discusses the history and development of the U.S. Air Force's
Spectre gunship, its design and special features, and some of the mis-
    sions it has flown in Vietnam, Panama, and in Kosovo in 1991.
    ISBN 0-516-23339-4 (lib. bdg.) – ISBN 0-516-23539-7 (pbk.)
    1. Spectre (Gunship)—Juvenile literature. 2. Gunships (Military air-
    craft)—United States—Juvenile literature.[1. Spectre (Gunship) 2.
    Gunships (Military aircraft)] I. Title.
    II. Series.

UG1242.G85 F58 2000
623.7'464—dc21
                                                                00-024380

CONTENTS

INTRODUCTION

The AC-130A Spectre gunship first appeared in the sky in 1967. This was during the Vietnam War (1965–1975). The U.S. Air Force built this attack plane by loading huge cargo planes with computers, machine guns, and cannons. To use these weapons effectively, special sensors were used to find the enemy on the ground. These high-tech military devices made the AC-130A a great success. This led to further production of this model, as well as later models: the AC-130E, AC-130H, and AC-130U.

Some of these models have seen their share of military action in the last ten years. In 1989-90, Spectres were used in Panama, a republic in the Caribbean, during Operation Just Cause. In 1991, they provided close air support to land troops in Kosovo, Yugoslavia.

The AC-130 Spectre has become a strong weapon against enemy ground troops in today's battlefields.

The AC-130A Spectre gunship first took to the air in 1967.

CHAPTER 1

THIS PLANE CAN FIGHT!

The AC-130 Spectre gunship is a huge plane. It was not designed to be a gunship at all. The AC-130 was a cargo plane called the C-130. As a cargo plane, it carried troops, weapons, vehicles, and bombs. In 1967, the U.S. Air Force decided to use the C-130 for a different purpose. They placed several cannons and machine guns inside the plane and began to use it against the enemy. The AC-130 is able to fly low and slow. This makes it a good fighting plane against targets on the ground. However, being so low and slow, the plane is open to enemy fire. That's why the Spectre

Spectre in the sky: the AC-130 in flight

gunship flies at night. If the enemy can't see it, then the plane is harder to hit.

With all its firepower and its size, the AC-130 Spectre became a huge success at destroying the enemy. How did it become successful so quickly? Why is it still a good fighting airplane thirty years later? There are many answers to these questions. The three most important reasons for its success are its firepower, its high-tech electronic equipment, and its ability to be changed as technology changes. During its thirty-year history, it has earned its mythic nickname, the "Fighting Herk."

A CARGO PLANE
TURNED INTO A GUNSHIP

A half-dozen cannons were bolted to the left side of a C-130 cargo plane. Some high-tech electronic equipment was added that would allow the crew to pinpoint targets as well as

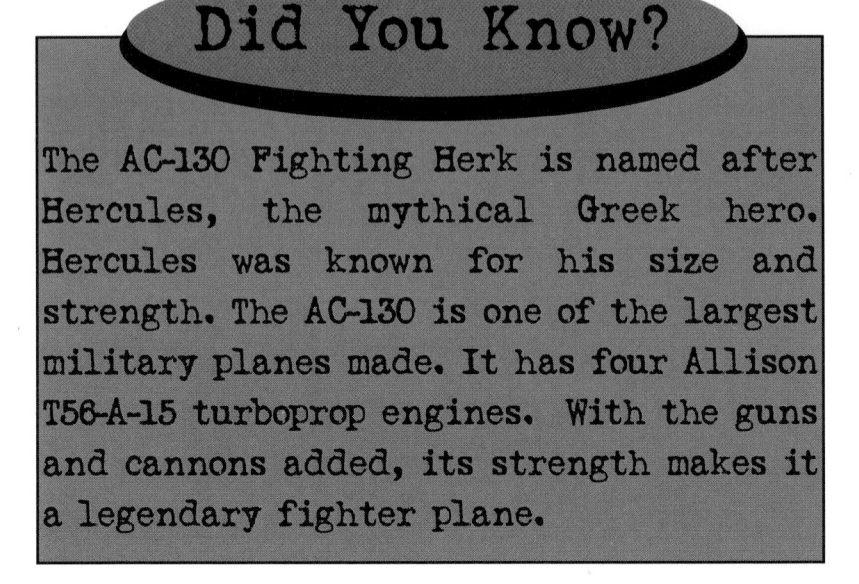

Did You Know?

The AC-130 Fighting Herk is named after Hercules, the mythical Greek hero. Hercules was known for his size and strength. The AC-130 is one of the largest military planes made. It has four Allison T56-A-15 turboprop engines. With the guns and cannons added, its strength makes it a legendary fighter plane.

steer the plane in the dark. These changes made a cargo plane into a flying battleship.

The Plane

The C-130 cargo plane is able to carry about 85,000 pounds. That's more than 40 tons! To be able to carry this weight, the plane has to be big. From wing tip to wing tip (wingspan), the C-130 measures 132 feet. The plane is 97 feet, 9 inches long, and 38 feet, 3 inches high. The C-130 is the size of half a football field.

When it was outfitted with its guns, cannons, and electronic equipment, the cargo plane became the AC-130 Spectre flying

gunship. The "A" was used to show that the plane was an attack plane.

What is special about the AC-130 is that it does not carry cargo. It is an attack plane. Except for its ammunition, guns, and crew, the plane flies empty. Flying light, the AC-130 has the ability to turn quickly and fly slower than such a big plane usually does. This allows the plane to fly its missions with greater success.

The AC-130 is an attack plane
specially made for battle.

MODIFIED GUNSHIPS

The AC-130 Spectre gunship has gone through many changes during its thirty years. Since this attack plane's creation, the United States has improved and perfected the AC-130. Each change has met the needs of the U.S. Air Force. The first Spectre flying gunship was given the letter "A" following its letter and number name. There have been many models since. They include the AC-130E, the AC-130C, the AC-130H, and the AC-130U.

These modified gunships are all improvements on the original model flown during the Vietnam War. Each is the result of changes made to weapons and electronic technology. These changes were needed so that the planes could compete against an enemy's improved technology. The AC-130 has developed into a more deadly and more powerful high-tech weapon.

CHAPTER 2

WEAPONS
AND
DEFENSE SYSTEMS

THE WEAPONS

All of the guns on any AC-130 stick out from the left side of the plane. This is because the plane flies in a pylon turn (circle) while it attacks its ground targets. Gunners fire repeatedly from inside that circle until the target is destroyed. The Spectre is the only plane in the world that attacks an enemy in this way.

Gatling Guns

Each AC-130 has two 20mm Gatling guns. The Gatling gun is a rapid-firing machine

The gunship comes armed to the teeth.

gun that has seven barrels. These barrels are fed bullets that fire from the gun at three-thousand rounds each minute. Such firepower can rip apart an enemy jeep, truck, or train as easily as you can tear apart a paper bag. After an attack from such guns, only chunks and pieces of a target remain.

Cannons

The AC-130 also has two different kinds of cannons. Cannons shoot a much larger bullet than does a gun. These bullets are called shells.

The Spectre has two 40-mm Bofors cannons. These cannons shoot a shell that is more than 1 1/2 inches wide. Cannons give the gunship an added firepower that allows it to fight against armored vehicles, buildings, and protected enemy positions.

The Spectre also has one 105-mm M102 Howitzer cannon. The Howitzer shell is more

than four inches wide. It can destroy an enemy tank.

With all these weapons, the flying gunship looks as if it can rip apart anything on the ground. It probably can. However, the plane does not simply fire blindly at the ground. That kind of plan only works if the enemy happens to be where the bullets and shells hit. Such an attack usually will end in failure. Instead, each AC-130 has special electronic equipment to "see" the enemy. Once seen,

The gunship has a 105-mm M102 Howitzer cannon.

the guns and cannons are aimed at the enemy. Once aimed, the weapons are fired and continue firing until the enemy has been destroyed.

THE SENSORS

The electronic equipment that each AC-130 Spectre carries includes scanners and sensors. These machines are as important to a successful mission as are the weapons. Some of these electronic devices help the crew to locate the enemy and aim the weapons. Others help the crew to keep the plane clear or safe from enemy ground fire.

FLIR and Side Radar

The forward looking infrared radar (FLIR) system helps the plane locate objects in front of the plane. Radar sends electronic signals into the air. These signals bounce off things that are in the air or on the ground. The

signals return to the radar instrument and show up on a video screen. Infrared radar is able to go through darkness, clouds, ice, and sand. Its ability to "see" through all kinds of weather helps the gunship find its targets.

AN/APG-180 "Strike" Radar

This radar is used to locate and lock onto enemy targets. Its signals search the ground for heat, movement, or electronic signals from enemy targets. Once found, the radar holds onto these targets electronically. When the Spectre locates an enemy and has it in its sights, it can begin firing its weapons at the target.

All-Light Level Television (ALLTV)

The ALLTV is another targeting sensor that locates an enemy target on the ground. This system is a television system that is able to see in the dark. Its sensors use the available light that the human eye cannot see. This light is used by the electronics to produce shapes on a video screen.

Fire Control System

The fire control system is an electronic system that aims the guns and cannons at the enemy target on the ground. This system is used by either the pilot or the fire control officer. They use this system when the enemy has been located by one of the radar systems. When the enemy is located and locked, the pilot or the fire control officer can aim the guns. They use an automatic aiming device that works with the gun sights. The guns are aimed at the ground targets onto which the radar screen has locked.

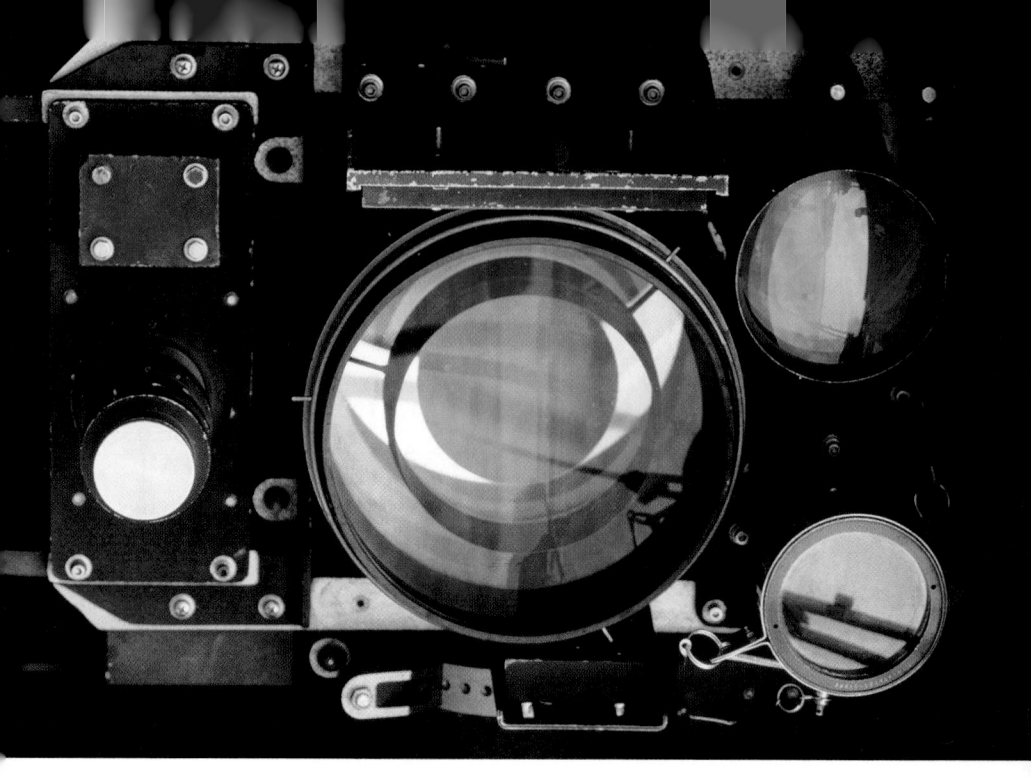

The AC-130 has special sensors
that help the crew to spot the enemy.

DEFENSIVE SYSTEMS

The AC-130 Spectre planes have electronic defensive systems to help them against enemy fire. One system finds and warns the crew that enemy radar is tracking them. The other system jams enemy radar.

Radar Homing and Warning

This device searches the electronic airwaves for enemy radar waves. An enemy might have

a radar station on the ground. This station can track the direction in which the Spectre is flying. When the Spectre is being tracked, the enemy radar operators can tell their own troops where to shoot at the plane.

Enemy radar also can come from a missile that has been shot at the Spectre. Some types of missiles use radar to lock onto and follow a target until it hits that target. This type of missile is a radar homing missile. The radar homing and warning device on Spectre gunships finds and warns the crew. The crew either can jam the missile's radar or shoot flares to attract its attention.

ALQ-172 Radar Jammer

This ALQ-172 radar jammer is used to interrupt enemy radar signals. Enemy radar becomes "jammed" when it can no longer track a target. The Spectre gunships can jam enemy radar stations that are ground-based.

The ALQ-172 radar jammer sits on the
left side of the nose of the Fighting Herk.

This allows the planes to circle and begin attacking without fear of being shot down.

The ALQ-172 also can jam radar homing missiles. When a missile's homing radar becomes jammed, it can no longer home in on the plane. However, there are times when the ALQ-172 cannot work properly. One reason for this failure is if a missile is heat-seeking. This kind of missile tracks and locks onto the heat produced by the plane's

engines. This kind of missile cannot be jammed. At this point, the plane must use its chaff.

Chaff and Flares

Radar homing, heat-seeking, and other missiles are used against aircraft. If a plane cannot jam radar signals, then chaff and flares are used. These defensive devices do not always work. However, they are better than having nothing at all to defend against an enemy.

Chaff is small metal pieces that are shot out the back of the plane as it flies. These metal fragments can make a missile miss a plane. This happens because the metal pieces attract the radar homing missile. Once the missile homes in on the chaff, it misses the plane. However, if a homing missile is too close to a plane, chaff will not work. This is because the metal that the plane is made of is a much better target for the missile than the small chaff.

The gunship can drop flares
to confuse enemy aircraft.

Flares are used against heat-seeking mis-siles. Flares are objects that burn brightly and hotly when set off. If a heat-seeking missile is far enough away from the plane, flares can be used. Flares send out enough heat to attract a missile that works by tracking the heat of a plane. Once a heat-seeking missile aims for the flares, the plane is safe.

CHAPTER 3

THE
SPECTRE GUNSHIP CREW

There are fourteen crew members aboard an AC-130 Spectre gunship. The plane is uncomfortable and loud. Crew members are crammed into small spaces. They are surrounded by electronic equipment and ammunition. Yet, somehow, the plane is able to fly to its target and destroy it. This happens because the crew works together as one unit to complete each mission.

PILOT AND COPILOT

The pilot and copilot sit in the cockpit. The pilot flies the plane and is the aircraft

The pilot and copilot sit in the gunship's cockpit.

commander. He has two important jobs. He flies the plane to and from the target, and he fires the weapons. The pilot receives his orders before the Spectre gunship takes off. He knows where the target is from these orders. He studies maps to learn the area over which he will fly. While the plane is in the air, the pilot directs the crew during the mission. They take orders from him and do their jobs as quickly as they can.

The pilot receives information about the enemy from "the booth." The booth is where

This AC-130 is getting ready for takeoff.

electronic experts sit in the plane and search for the enemy. They use the electronic radar equipment. When the enemy position is located, the pilot circles the area. As the plane circles the target, the pilot orders other crew members to load the guns. When the guns are ready, the pilot can aim the guns at the targets and shoot.

The copilot helps the pilot fly the plane. He also acts as a spotter by scanning the ground for signs of the enemy. The copilot also can fly the plane if the pilot is unable to fly it during the mission.

THE BOOTH

The booth is directly behind the cockpit. The three crew members inside the booth are surrounded by electronic equipment. Their offensive and defensive radar scans the air and the ground as the plane flies toward its target. The electronic war officer (EWO)

watches over two sensor operators. The sensor operators give the EWO information about the target and the target area. The EWO then relays this information to the pilot. The pilot uses such information to begin the Spectre's attack. Some information may cause the pilot to break off the attack.

THE GUN DECK CREW

The gun deck sits behind the booth. The gun deck is a long, wide compartment that holds the guns. These machine guns and cannons face the left side of the plane. On the right side is stored the ammunition that is loaded into the guns and cannons.

The gun deck crew includes a right scanner and the weapons crew. The right scanner looks through a window at the ground. Like the copilot, he scans the ground for enemy position and the position of the Spectre. The gunship must be in a proper position to fire

The gun deck crew is responsible for loading the gunship's weapons.

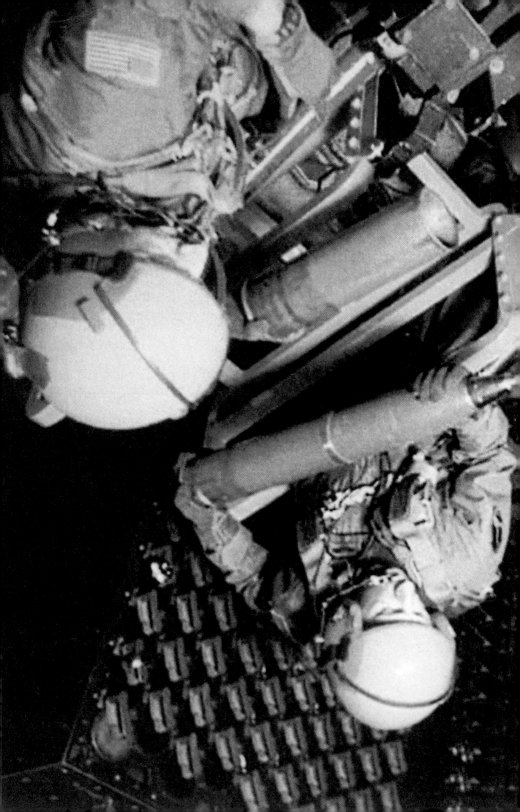

its guns. As already explained, the AC-130 Spectres fly in a pylon position. This circle route is used to allow the guns to fire constantly at the target.

The weapons crew maintains the readiness of the guns and cannons. This crew does not fire the weapons. Instead, they make sure that the guns are loaded and firing properly. As the guns and cannons fire, the weapons crew feed them more ammunition. If a shell gets stuck while firing, a member of the weapons crew clears the jam. Once clear, the gun can continue firing.

During their firing, the guns and cannons spit out used shells. The weapons crew uses shovels to pick up all this "brass." They store these used shells in canvas bags. The shells will be recycled for a future mission.

During combat, all AC-130 Spectre crews are in danger. They fly missions to fight an enemy. You can be sure that the enemy is

fighting back as best it can. If the Spectre crews work together and do their jobs properly, they have a great chance of completing their missions. A successful mission means that they have destroyed the enemy and returned to base safely.

Watch out—the gunship is on the attack!

CHAPTER 4

COMBAT OPERATIONS

For more than thirty years, AC-130 Spectre gunships have been a huge part of protecting ground troops and attacking slow-moving targets (such as troop and cargo trucks and trains). What follows is a description of how the plane operates during a mission and where the plane has been used.

VIETNAM

The AC-130 Spectre gunship played an important part in the Vietnam War. Its crew was in the air to destroy trucks, troops, and anything else that was coming across the

The Spectre gunship can be used to drop cargo for troops on land.

dividing line between South Vietnam and communist North Vietnam. Spectres were very successful on such missions.

Later in the war, the Spectre was used to help ground troops move through enemy positions. It also was used to destroy enemy buildings and troops. During this time, the Spectre began to gain more respect with the military because of its great success. The

The U.S. military used the gunship during the Gulf War (1991).

military began to put better guns and cannons on the ship. Then it could destroy larger and more powerful enemy positions.

GRENADA AND PANAMA

During the 1980s, the Spectre gunship continued to see action in places such as Grenada (Operation Urgent Fury) and Panama (Operation Just Cause). The planes were used to fire on the enemy while U.S. troops and other friendly troops were close by. There isn't another aircraft in the world that can fire so close to its own troops and still hit the enemy.

1990s CONFLICTS

In the 1990s, the Spectre gunship saw even more combat. During the Gulf War (1991) and in Somalia (Operation Restore Hope, 1992), the gunship flew combat missions that helped friendly troops to attack the enemy.

They were successful in helping friendly troops move and in targeting and destroying enemy troops and facilities.

Most recently, AC-130 gunships were used in Kosovo. Kosovo is a region of Yugoslavia that was at civil war. Serbians were killing ethnic Albanians. The United States and other countries saw that the Albanians living in Kosovo needed help. The Albanians began to leave Kosovo as war refugees. In 1999, the U.S. Air Force used AC-130 Spectre gunships to stop the Serbians from harming the Albanian refugees. The planes circled enemy ground troops and fired on them. Such missions allowed thousands of Albanians to flee Kosovo unharmed.

BATTLE LOSSES

The Spectre flying gunships have not been perfect during their missions. A Spectre was shot down six times during the Vietnam War

This AC-130 dropped flares over Kosovo.

An AC-130 in flight is a beautiful sight!

by enemy fire. During the Gulf War, one gunship was shot down. In Somalia, a Spectre crashed when some of its ammunition exploded. Eight of its fourteen crew members died in this accident.

As you can see, combat is dangerous. However, the AC-130 Spectre has had great success at not getting shot down during its missions. Several things have allowed this plane to be so successful. The Spectre flies its

missions at night. The Spectre fires many guns and cannons at its target all the time it is in the air circling the target. The Spectre also has defensive electronic equipment. These are the three most important parts of this plane's defense.

THE FUTURE OF THE FIGHTING HERK

If the history of the Spectre gunship has taught us anything, it's that the planes need to be adaptable. Wherever the mission, the AC-130 Spectre gunships have been there. Their readiness and firepower have saved civilians and friendly troops. Whether in the jungle of Southeast Asia, the desert in the Middle East or, most recently, in Europe and the crisis in Kosovo, this aircraft has adjusted and succeeded in its mission.

You can be sure of one thing. The AC-130 Spectres will continue to develop as technology becomes better.

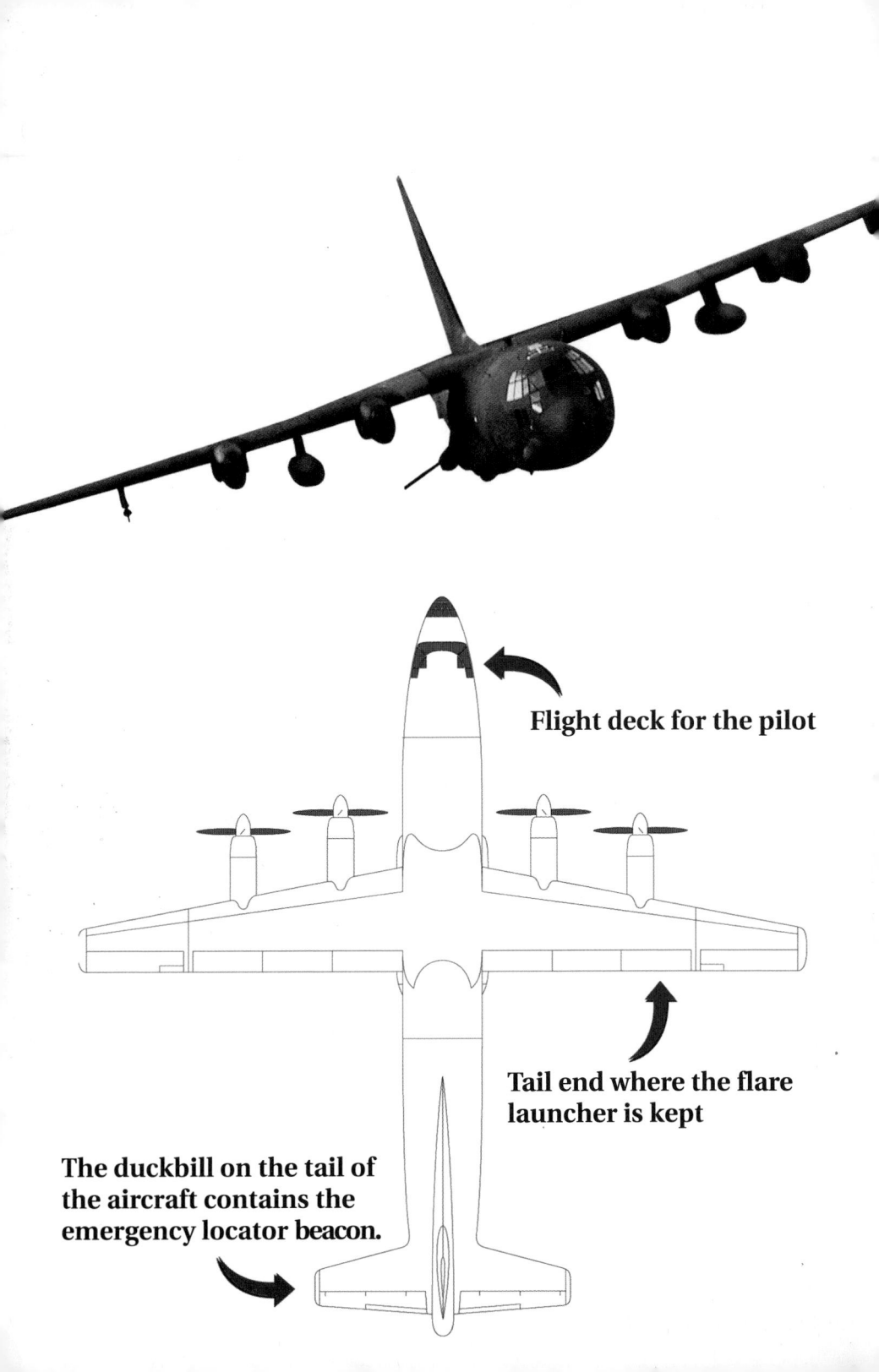

Flight deck for the pilot

Tail end where the flare launcher is kept

The duckbill on the tail of the aircraft contains the emergency locator beacon.

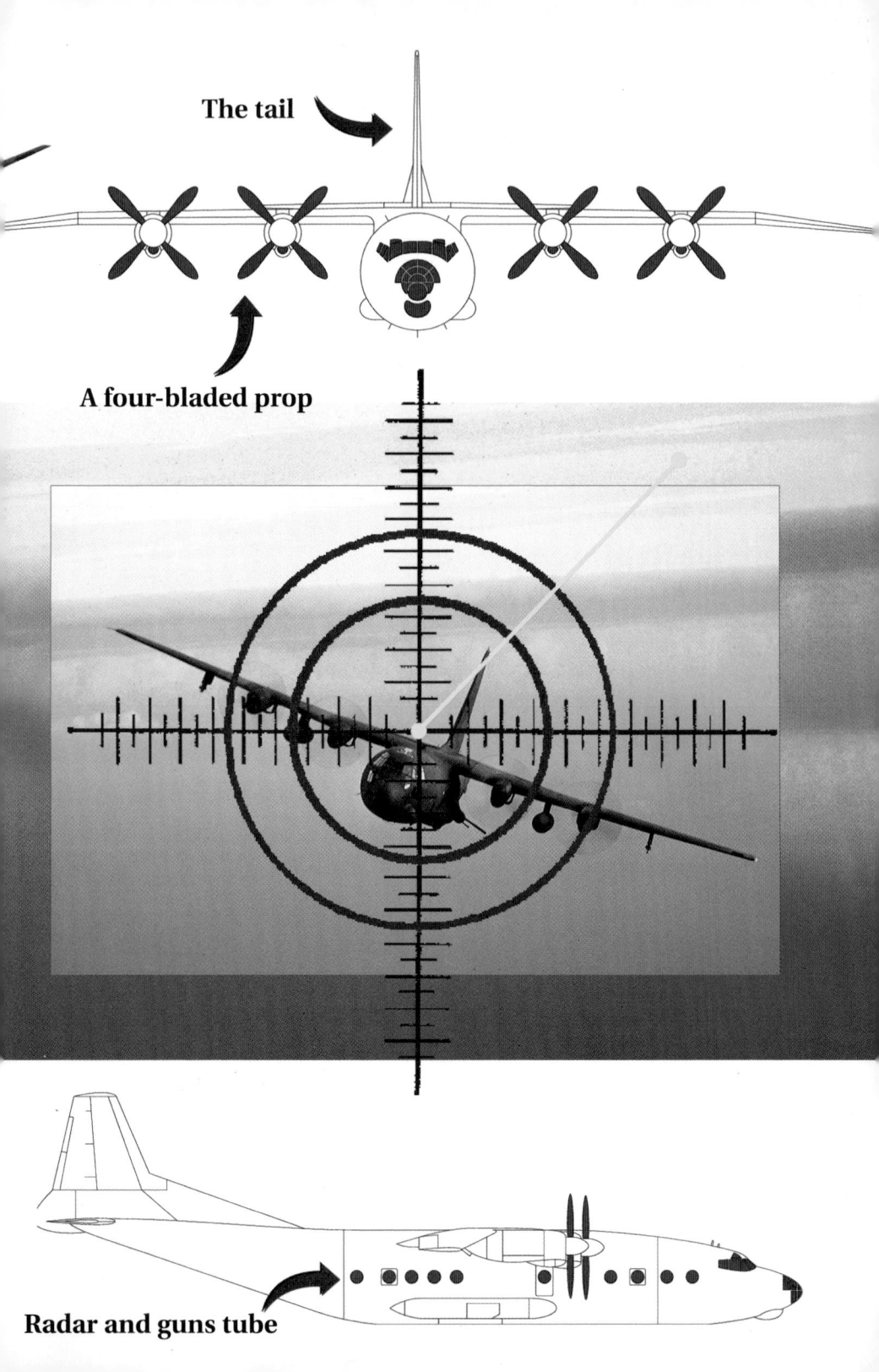

The tail

A four-bladed prop

Radar and guns tube

ammunition bullets and explosives that are
fired from guns and cannons

brass outer covers of ammunition

cargo goods that are carried by trains,
planes, and trucks

chaff metal pieces shot from behind planes
to interrupt homing missiles

flares objects that burn brightly and hotly
to interrupt heat-seeking missiles

gunship an airplane that has machine guns
and cannons fixed to it

homing going to the place or thing at which
something is aimed

Howitzer a short cannon that fires large
bullets

infrared radar electronic detection device
that can be used in all kinds of weather

jam to be stuck or caught on something

NEW WORDS

legendary a person or thing with a history that people believe

missile a rocket that carries a bomb to someplace

mission a task that people are sent to complete

mythic a made-up story that tells something about life

pinpoint to aim at something in an exact spot

pylon turn a circular turn that a plane makes

radar (RAdio Detection And Ranging) an electronic device that locates objects in the air and on the ground

sensors a device that sends a signal when it captures light, sound, heat, or pressure

shells ammunition

FOR FURTHER READING

Blue, Rose, and Corrine J. Naden. *The U.S. Air Force*. Brookfield, CT: Millbrook Press, Incorporated, 1994.

Gunston, Bill. *Fighter Planes*. Hauppauge, NY: Barron's Juveniles, 1999.

Lowe, Malcolm V., Peter Sarson, and Tony Bryan. *Fighters*. Minneapolis, MN: The Lerner Publishing Group, 1985.

Jay Schleifer. *Fighter Planes*. Danbury, CT: Children's Press, 1998.

RESOURCES

Air Force Recruiting Station – Midwest
536 S. Clark Street, Room 279
Chicago, IL 60605
(312) 663-1640

Air Force Recruiting Station – Northeast
43rd Street & Broadway
New York, NY 10036
(212) 575-0080

Air Force Recruiting Station – South
9245 Skillman Avenue, Suite 103C
Dallas, TX 75243
(214) 341-7266

Air Force Recruiting Station – West
3207 South Hoover Street, Unit B7
Los Angeles, CA 90007
(213) 748-6105

RESOURCES

Web Sites
The AC130 Gunship
http://home.imcnet.net/%7Ekrstofer/newa-sos/ac130.htm
This site explains the features and background of the AC-130 gunship. It also provides a history of the use of the plane.

Air Force Link
www.af.mil/index.html
The official site of the U.S. Air Force. View pictures and learn what its primary missions are. It includes details of the plane's special features.

The Aviation Zone
www.TheAviationZone.com
This site provides a history of the gunship. It also includes an extensive image gallery and links to other aviation sites.

INDEX

INDEX

About the Author

Kevin J. Fitzpatrick received his B.A. in English from the University of Illinois and his M.F.A. in Creative Writing from Columbia College. He currently lives in Chicago where he teaches writing at both DePaul and Loyola Universities.